Programmed Sheep

Do You Control Your Mind or does Somebody Else Control It for You?

Programmed Sheep

Do You Control Your Mind or does Somebody Else Control It for You?

BY

M. A. Fricker

Strategic Book Publishing and Rights Co.

Strategic Book Publishing and Rights Co.
12620 FM 1960, Suite A4-507
Houston TX 77065
www.sbpra.com

ISBN: 978-1-62212-903-4

Dedicated to
The world of the stressed and unappreciated hard-workers of
the modern world.

'I'm only saying what you're thinking'

'Time to use your own mind instead of believing everything
that is fed to you'
You *can* be in control of your own life again. Now, wouldn't
that be good?

Open your eyes, use your heads and, most of all, THINK,
because 'The power of thought is everything'.

MAF

CONTENTS

CHAPTER ONE
STRESSED OUT NATION   **1**
    Stressed?   2
    Cost of living   5
    You're An Insignificant Sheep   13
    False Hope and Ambition   18
    Television   25
    Retirement and Debt   27

CHAPTER TWO
MIDLIFE CRISIS   **38**
    The Signs   39
    A Dictatorship   50
    Welfare state   62

CHAPTER THREE
BASTARDS   **67**
    Charity   75
    Fucked-up Britain   78
    S.A.D.   82
    Bad Apples   83

CHAPTER FOUR
PROGRAMMING THE SHEEP   88

    Introduction   89

    Sport—herding the sheep   108

    We are all followers and we need to be led   111

    Programming For Conformist Sperms   115

    What is a true conformist sheep?   121

    A Typical Day For A Programmed Working Class Sheep

    Things a programmed conformist is most likely to
        get up to before they go to bed.

A WARNING FROM THE AUTHOR:

Read carefully before you continue.
(This book contains a lot of explicit sexual swear words)

I hereby claim diminished responsibility for the contents of this book, as I was somewhat not of sound mind when I wrote it.

I also apologise if any of the contents offend you. It wasn't my intention. It was written for entertainment purposes only, and basically my chance to have a bloody good rant and put my feelings and philosophies and observations about day-to-day life as I see it to you.

I strongly advise you not to let young children get their hands on it, as this is not a children's book.

And as for any students that are studying English literature, this book will do you no good whatsoever in your studies on the English language.

M A Fricker
MAF

PREFACE

I call the book *Programmed Sheep* basically because of my observation that it seems we humans are programmed to work and behave like sheep, and we are therefore being treated as such by the government, politicians, employers and the police alike. And rather than just following the flock, I wanted to break free for a while and make you all aware of this, too. I want to show you that you are an individual, a free thinker, and you don't have to keep going in the direction the politicians are directing you to go all the time. So throughout this book, I will refer to the politicians as your 'Shepherds'.

I want you to open your eyes to the greed of these corporate companies, the corrupt government representatives and dodgy bankers, not forgetting the politically correct brigade who, together, have contributed to systematically destroying your true identity as a human.

Also, it seems to me that all of our values and traditions of long ago, like festivals, street parties, garden parties and such like, what we refer to as 'the good old days', the ones which brought communities together, have now been taken from us. These days, if we want fun we have to pay for it. You know as well as I do, if there is a festival on anywhere it's all about making money from us sheep. This is more apparent here in my home country of Great Britain than anywhere; you can't have any fun unless you are prepared to pay for it. In Britain, if there is no financial gain for the government, you're not allowed to have any free fun. Free fun seems to have been banished from this land forever. You're talking to a guy who remembers when the Glastonbury festival used to be free—now it costs a small fortune just to get in.

I feel most of the people—sorry, sheep—of this country are, at the moment, feeling lost; we've lost all hope and faith in the future of this once great land of ours. Money seems to rule, and apathy has taken over. But ignorance isn't a cure my friend, is it? A realisation that you're being fleeced may turn things around.

The Olympics was a money-making venture, as most events like it are; and remember, its success was achieved from the hard work of you sheep. It just goes to show, if we all work together we can achieve great things. But for fuck's sake, why did you do it for free? You 'volunteered' to help with the Olympics. Why, for fuck's sake? For a nice uniform, a nice T-shirt to make you feel special… you stupid sheep! Why did you volunteer? None of the stars you saw volunteered, did they? And as far as I was concerned, you fuckers were more entertaining than them. Mind you, I did find Mr Bean funny.

One thing that did come out of the success of the Olympics— at least, here in Britain, anyway—is that it may kick-start us all to have more faith in ourselves as a nation. Morale did pick up somewhat, together with the Queen's coronation. 2012 was a good year for the people of Britain; just a shame about the weather.

Hopefully, the good year we had may even spark the next generation to turn their computers, televisions and mobile phones off, and go out and mix with other sheep and start being less anti-social. To basically start having fun together again, out in the fresh air. Let's clear our lungs from this stagnant, negative air spewed out by listening to politicians and religious nuts talk shit, and listen to our own minds and hearts. Listen to nature for a change, and the laughter of people having fun. Once again, let's start to enjoy the open air again, people. Maybe it will inspire us all to be as great as we all can be, rather than acting like sheep and focusing on the negative all the time.

Our shepherds of the government and the prime ministers and presidents (the farmers) of the world have kept you penned in for too long. It's alright for them, they were born wealthy; for them, most things landed in their lap because they are the privileged. Most of them live their hunky-dory lives because of your hard work, remember that. They live in a fairytale world.

The *real* world out there is the one me and you live in, and it isn't like that at all. I'm a simple, working-class sheep and I can see the shithole this world is becoming, and it's all because of selfishness and greed. Sheep don't mind working, generally—if, of course, they can see the benefits of doing so, and if they are lucky enough to hold a job at all. Those of you who do work, I bet most of you don't enjoy having to do so; this is because most sheep are forced into jobs they don't particularly like—and, may I add, for piss poor pay, too. This is why we are all so unhappy and less keen to work hard and so less productive; the more we do, the more the fuckers want. The more we earn, the more they take.

MICKY FRICK'S TIP

GIVE YOURSELF A MENTAL PAY RISE. IF, SAY, YOU'RE ON £10 AN HOUR IN AN 8-HOUR DAY, GIVE YOURSELF A £10 POUND RISE. NOW YOU ARE ON £20 A HOUR AND ONLY GIVE THEM WORK EQUIVALENT TO 4 HOURS.

If you shepherds and farmers want to understand the reasons behind the riots of August 2011, maybe you should start listening to what every young sheep is saying to you for once. Even though I really don't condone riots, I do understand why they may have happened. The simple answer is frustration; you have brainwashed the kids—sorry, our lambs—to want for material things, yet you as a piss poor government have offered these sheep no future prospects of ever finding work to fund what it is they want. Well, that's what I reckon, anyway.

What chances do us sheep have if the shepherd is blind?
MAF

I'm a British sheep, and I think that British sheep have put up with enough shit from our so-called politicians (shepherds). Their job is to report back to the farm and let the Prime Minister (the farmer) know what the sheep are feeling, but they don't seem to hear what we are saying. Basically, they don't give a toss. We see what they are doing, wasting our taxes and pocketing what's left for themselves; but they seem oblivious to the detrimental effect it is having on our lives, so what chance do us sheep have if the shepherd is blind? Shepherds think they know what's best for us, yet they know fuck all about keeping sheep; it's been going on for far too long now and we, the flock, have had enough. We are fed up with constantly being fleeced by you.

As a working sheep, I feel let down and betrayed by the shepherds and the farmer of this country, because they don't realise the working class sheep of this world are and always will be the lifeline of everything. You need happy, productive sheep who are fit and healthy, both physically and mentally. They need to feel they have a purpose and are useful to the whole flock; they also want to be appreciated and rewarded for their efforts. They do say 'A happy work force is a productive workforce', yet we working class sheep of Britain—especially me—are not happy, not happy at all. The farmer and the shepherds need to understand this, or else we will all go down.

This book has been written in a totally unique style. I say this, because I'm not a clever sheep, so therefore my book may include bad grammar and poor punctuation; it may also contain un-intellectual comments. Basically, I tend to move my mouth before my mind is in gear. Oh well, I am as I am. So what? Why should I follow the flock?

I guess you could say I may well be the world's first un-conformist sheep to write a book of this kind. Yes, I still am a little like a sheep, even now. However, I don't like being treated as a sheep, so because of this I can now recognise when I am doing it and stop myself. Like, sometimes I will go a different route to work, or don't go to work at all; I'll have the odd day off, or just do something completely spontaneous, like yesterday, when I grabbed my wife and made love to her on the kitchen floor. Marvellous. J

Even this book was spontaneous; one day, I just decided to jump the fence to try and find my own identity, as a form of self-therapy if you like. As far as I'm aware, never has any book like this one been published before, so I guess you could say this is a literal revolution. Well, not many sheep can type.

So, I am going to be your spokesperson/sheep and speak on behalf of all us working sheep of the world. I will help you break away from the flock and then you can stand alone as a freethinking individual for a while and realise how amazing you really are.

Now. *You* can read this book or bin it, I don't really give a toss anymore. It's entirely up to you. It's your choice. However, I do hope that you decide to stick with it to the bitter end, because I believe the contents are, well, 'eye opening' if nothing else; it may open your mind to what's really going on in the world around you and make you realise you're not alone in your thinking.

This book, my friend, can become very addictive. Whilst you are entering *my* strange and wonderful mind, you will undoubtedly be engrossed by the poetry I grace your brain with; and as your mind wonders in a dream-like status and the rainbow of colourful language titillates your every being, suddenly it will open your eyes and mind—even your soul—to what is really going on in the field. Eventually, you will feel spiritually alive again and, hopefully, after this journey together, you, me and every sheep who reads this wonderful book of mine will become as one. Together, with a bit of luck, we can save the world from these delusional farmers and shepherd and begin using our own free will and start directing *them* for a change.

The message is simple:

Fucking baaa! to the establishment!

INTRODUCTION

Hello and Welcome to you from me, 'THE UN-CONFORMIST SPIRITUAL ANARCHIST SHEEP'.

Firstly, let me introduce myself. My name is Michael A. Fricker, but my friends call me Micky Fricker. I live in the lush green land we like to call Great Britain and I, as far as I'm aware, apart from my Grandfather's brother E.G. Fricker (known as Ted), the world-famous healer, am the only other Sheep in our family for generations to ever write a book. Ted was made famous by healing or simply bringing relief to millions of sheep of their physical ailments. Although I am not a healer like he was, I do have a certain gift bestowed upon me by God—no, I can't see into the future, or help sheep with their pain. My gift is being able to make sheep laugh. I have had this gift from birth, but most recently I have discovered I have been blessed with another gift, the gift to make sheep understand a bit more about who they are and why they exist. I have the key to open up your minds to understand what life is really all about, and your purpose in life.

The non-believers out there see me simply as a nutcase. Sometimes, I think they might be right; but they do say, if you think you're mad, you're probably not. So maybe I'm not.

So… putting the small introduction of myself to one side, welcome once again and thank you very much for deciding to buy my book. Knowing we all live in a busy world, all trying to earn a living, I thought no sheep is ever going to have the time to read an epic; and, if you're anything like me, if I don't stick with a book and read a chapter every day, I lose the plot—or, in my case, I forget where I was, and soon get bored. Hence the reason why I have split this book into two—part two of this book is called *Paranoid Sheep* and will be out soon.

In these two small, easy-to-read books you will finally gain an understanding of yourself, the way the world works and, most importantly, how to make your life better than it is right now. I think I've done the right thing. I hope you agree. Once you have finished this book, hopefully you'll buy the second one, which ties everything together, and you will then understand how I got to my overall conclusions of the meaning of life—according to me, that is.

At the moment, I feel more enlightened than ever before and quite happy my life has changed ten-fold, and I want to help you feel the same. There is a chance you may just end up thinking, 'No, he's a nutter', but I'll entertain you for a while if nothing else with my moaning and ranting, together with my wacky thoughts and mad sense of humour, all of which are incorporated within these books. Hopefully, I'll make it an enjoyable read for you. I am sure you will find it, if nothing else, entertaining; besides, you've got nothing to lose. If it isn't as good as I think it is, you can eat it. Mind you, if you're using a Kindle that isn't advisable—you're not a goat.

I am not here to try to convert your way of thinking or persuade you to join a sheep cult of any kind, you understand, such as becoming a Buddha sheep, Jehovah Witness sheep or Mormon sheep, or what have you. I am not a strange alien sheep from another planet, and neither have I been abducted, as far as I know... Come to think of it, there was this one time... No, forget it—I'm nothing special at all. I'm not even a psychopathic lunatic or devil worshiper. The fact is, I'm just a simple, ordinary, everyday working-class sheep, much like most of the population of the world, and I have basically decided to write a book. That's it, nothing more. Well, some sheep do, don't they? If they can type.

Now, listen to me because this is very important. Throughout this book you will see what I call 'Micky Frick's Tips'; these will help you get your own back on the bastards who control your life. Look out for them, as these will help you hold on to your individuality. I refer to them every day.

MICKY FRICKS TIP

I TELL MYSELF I AM SPECIAL EVERY DAY. YOU SHOULD DO THE SAME.

I really do feel a deep-down, burning need to share all I am with you. So, by bonding and bringing our minds together, I believe we can make this world a better place—hopefully.

In *Programmed Sheep,* I released all this built-up frustration that I have harboured all my sorry life and allow myself a bloody good rant. Then it all changes in book two, when I calm down a bit. This is because I soon get a better understanding of what's really going on in the world, and I start to put some sense to all the crap. I found, after blowing away all the cobwebs in my mind, that it left me open to fully understand what I believe to be the answers to many of the unanswered questions that we all, at some time in our lives, have asked ourselves. For instance: What is the point? Why am I here? There must be more to life?

There *is* more to life. Now, listen up, my fellow sheep— the knowledge I obtained from years of painstaking research on almost every topic imaginable was done so you don't have to, okay? What I didn't expect was to stumble on some interesting and sometimes disturbing topics that affect us all in everyday life, which we are kept in the dark about, or so it seems; so bad, in fact, that they changed my entire view on life completely and made me think more intensely about stuff. I was thinking, 'Okay, what else are they not telling us? And Why?' I even became paranoid for a while. Hence book two's title, *Paranoid Sheep*. However, I am okay now, more an optimist sheep deep down, and even I think we still have a slim chance of surviving it all. I think I've worked it all out, and hopefully I'm going to be able to pass on my wisdom to you.

If you do decide to continue on this quest to understand life according to me, to fully understand how I came to my overall conclusion of the meaning of life and, more important, how to *live* your life, you must be prepared to read both books, and don't waste any time either according to them clever sheep out there. We haven't got long, so we need to start changing things soonish.

I am, these days, more a spiritual sheep. This is because I underwent a physical change in my personality whilst writing my books; all my stress slowly disappeared as I wrote and, regardless of what I discovered, it didn't seem to matter anymore. It just seemed that, page after page, all my frustrations gradually faded away as I got closer to my overall conclusion of the meaning of life. Like, for instance, at the beginning of this book you will notice I swear, well… quite a lot. This is because I write from the heart.

When I started this book back in the year 2000, I was run-down, depressed, and basically pissed off with life. But, over the years, I have learnt to laugh it off, and you will too in the end. You've got to, or you will forever be a miserable fucker as I was, restless and lost in a world of crap. But, I will tell you this; you will discover that it's all bollocks at the end of the day and life is too short to worry about shit that may never happen. It's the year 2012 now and I'm no longer as stressed as I was. I now have a bit more compassion and understanding towards people who don't know they are sheep, and I try and bring it to their attention whenever I can. Hopefully, my experiences will help you find your true identity.

I know I can't change the world by myself, but collectively, as a flock, I think we could make this world a better place—if we wanted to, that is. If nothing else, I guarantee you will start to think freely again instead of being directed by the farmers of the world, as such. So come on, let's start airing our lungs and stand up to the delusional sheep in power. You have a voice, use it. Baaa as loud as you can at the bastards.

I am your Guru sheep—I'm not as mad as people think.

Mind you, there is still a good chance I could flip at a moment's notice, but if I do at least you will understand why. But for now, before you start worrying about my mental health, you firstly need to understand your own mind, Most of us don't understand our own minds—you think you do, but you really don't. Trust me on this one.

Do you control your mind or does somebody control it for you?

I start my journey back in the year 2000 when I was very stressed, a lost sheep in fact. I wasn't sure what I was doing with my life. However, by the end of book two, I ended up a totally enlightened, even spiritual, person. What you are about to read are my thoughts as they were back in 2000.

'I am a genius, I'm just not a very clever one'

MAF

Are you sitting comfortably? Then I shall begin.
Enjoy.

PROGRAMMED SHEEP

'What chances do us sheep have if the Shepherd's blind?'

MAF

CHAPTER ONE

STRESSED-OUT NATION

'The reason I believe we are such a stressed-out nation is simply because, if we consider life to be one big show, we can't be true to ourselves because we all play the roles that are given to us in this show. So how can we truly shine if we don't like the part we are stuck with?'

MAF

Stressed?

If, when you are woken up by your alarm clock, the first words out of your mouth are 'Oh bollocks', then you rub the sleep from your crusted eyes, stretch, fart, and then make a move to get out of your warm bed, whilst listening to the radio as some twat tells you the cost of living is going up, and you still get ready for your job—which you hate—then, my friend, you are already suffering from that mental illness called stress. I am probably going to have a bit of a challenge on my hands to help you out of it, but laughing helps.

I hope I'm not too late to save you from the conformist conditioning and brain-washing you have been subjected to all your sorry life, which has turned you into the programmed working sheep you are today. I may even be able to help you fight back to retain your identity, your individuality that you once had; I may even be able to help you combat that stress and get you to start thinking positively again which, in turn, will make it easier for you to get out of that warm bed each morning to go to your job. I'll give it my best shot, anyway, regardless of the fact you are just a dumb sheep.

MONDAY 10th January 2000

GOOD MORNING Britain—and the world, come to that. Yes, it's Monday again, you poor lost sheep. How you feeling today? Christmas has come and gone, we all survived the millennium, but now you are feeling pissed off I bet. So here we go again, eh? After your traditional shit, shave, and shower, it's time to start yet another monotonous, boring, unappreciated week of work. I guess you already have that sinking feeling in the pit of your stomach at the thought of going to that shithole once again, don't you? It's natural to feel that way.

This mundane routine of life you are stuck with is a real burden, and it's the same all around the world. What is it that makes us bother? I mean, you have a cuppa, maybe a bite to eat, then you look up at the clock and think about your commute to work and that dreaded rush hour traffic you have to face; but, like a fucking robot, we just go with the routine regardless, don't we?

Every sheep who works for a living across the planet feels how you feel right now—subdued and knackered. Usually, you don't wake up fully until you are sitting in your car, I bet. The sheep in the car next to you is feeling just the same. Pissed off. You're thinking, "There must be more to life', but the reason you are stuck in that traffic, off to work as always, is simple: You have been programmed to do it. You have been programmed to fucking work.

MICKY FRICK'S TIP

I NOW TAKE DIFFERENT ROUTES TO WORK. YOU SHOULD DO THE SAME.

Mondays… Monday must be the most miserable fucking day of the week, I reckon. Friday seems to be so fucking far away and the weekends are so short. I don't know why it is, but Mondays to me always seem to be raining. Do you know, I think the rain is when the heavens are crying in sympathy for us all. Mondays. I really fucking hate Mondays, I do. Does my gripe sound like you? Well, I'll tell you why, shall I? You're stressed. You have the 'Working Class Blues'. You have a right to be stressed. After all, working for a living is wank.

I work here in the 'United Kingdom', this once great empire of ours, which is now buckling at the knees, as most of the free world is. The reason for that is because it's being run by greedy, corporate companies. Here in Britain, at the moment we are being overwhelmed by asylum seekers stealing our jobs and, as if to rub salt in our wounds, they are either being given handouts by a government using our tax money, or working for a pittance so the greedy employers won't need to employ British people anymore. It's cheaper to employ beggars, *and* they work harder than us, so they say. My heart goes out to anybody who can't get a job. I'm lucky, I still have a job; but as unemployment grows worse in this country, I can see, sooner or later, the shit will really hit the fan.

Soon, British-born workers will be in the minority in this country and unemployment and frustration could spark unruly behaviour, riots even. This is because, just lately, it seems everywhere you look there are less and less jobs, and so people are getting angry. Our very own government is turning its back on its own people and letting these foreigners come into this country in their droves and slowly taking over our land. It's not just in this country, either; it's happening all across the world. Stressed, of course. You're fucking stressed.

MICKY FRICK'S TIP

REMEMBER, YOU'RE NOT ON YOUR OWN IN YOUR THINKING AND FEELINGS

However, I can offer you this small piece of comfort. You're not on your own. I would warrant a guess that most of the British working class—in fact, the world's working class, come to that—are stressed just like you are. Times are getting hard.

Do you know, I wouldn't be surprised if the British working class are the most stressed-out people in Europe. The more we earn, the more they take. That's why Britain is one of the most expensive countries to live in. I mean, we work more hours than any other bastard in the world and then, at the end of the week, we pick up insufficient pay for the cost of living here; in fact, it's barely enough to pay the ever increasing bills to live basic lives. This truly is rip-off Britain. No wonder we are stressed. Our own government is ripping its own people off for living here. Wankers, the lot of them.

Cost Of Living

It's a joke, what with a mortgage, water rates, electric, gas, telephone bills, etc, etc. Fuck knows how they work them out. They are all ripping us off, you know. They use impossible mathematics so you can't see how they are doing it. Like your electricity bill—what's that all about, for fuck's sake? You need to be a mathematician to work that out. They make me sick—the bill is so difficult for you to understand, you don't really know how much they're ripping you off—the fucking wankers. What I do know is I'm getting poorer every year because of them bastards. Fuck me, I hardly have enough money left to spend on myself, and if they keep taking money from me as the do soon I won't even be able to afford a visit the dentist before long. I'll probably be pulling my own teeth out with a plastic spoon.

A basic haircut. Ha! That in itself would be a luxury. Talking about luxuries, a car is a luxury, but look at the running costs of a car—the insurance, MOTs, road tax. Road tax rip-off! The sole purpose of the road tax was to cover the costs of fixing up the roads, to keep them in good useable order, or am I mistaken? Well, going to work the other day, my head was bouncing up and down like a headbanger having a fit there were that many potholes. Now the fuckers are bringing in toll roads everywhere. And do you think will we get that refunded on the road tax? Will we bollocks, the robbing bastards. This is literally highway robbery of the modern world, my friend. You don't need a bloke in a mask pointing a gun at your face shouting 'Stand and deliver'. They've set up toll booths now, instead. What the fuck is going on, hey? I won't ever use a toll, that's a promise. Fuck 'em, they can go and kiss my arse.

It's getting worse in this country. Do you know what they have got on the agenda now? I'll tell you. Congestion charges in every city across Britain—not just London. That was just a trial, mark my words. We'll have congestion charges right across the land before long. But that's what they want—

congestion charges; this means you will have to pay to go into every city in England, so if you work in a city you're going to be fucked once again. It's going to get so bad that, one day, you will have to pay to go to work in the first place. Fuck off! It should be the other way around, shouldn't it? They are really taking the piss—robbing bastards. So, you can understand why we, the drivers, are all pissed off and why there is so much road rage. We are paying that much to use the road we feel we own it.

Yep, cars are the biggest rip-off there is, because they know full well we need one to get about. It's alright saying try not to use your car whenever possible, but if I did that I would have to walk to work. Fuck that! For one, there isn't a bus that stops outside my work, so I would have to walk it there, and I'm not going to do that, am I? By doing that, I would have to start out about two and a half hours earlier, just so that I would get to work on time, and by the time I got there I would be too fucking knackered to any work. No, they're not stupid, you know—they know you're not going to walk to work. They are fully aware we need our motors, so there you go. They've got us all over a barrel. You have got to give it to them—what a great way to generate revenue for the fat cat club, the robbing bastards.

I don't know, what *is* the world coming to? We are all just pissing in the wind with this bunch of twats. Have you noticed, it's all them Twats, with a capital T, who have the money that introduce these wonderful ideas? They can afford it, but we fucking can't. It doesn't affect them, see. It's just the likes of you and me, who can barely scrape a living, that get affected by the things they come up with. The same can be said whenever we try to improve our lifestyle; we save a bit, but then just as we seem to be chugging along nicely some fucker knocks us back down again, two steps forward three steps back (the dance of life).

Well, that's it. I for one have had enough. No more 'Shall I take this crap?' NO FUCKING MORE! We have let the 'wankers' of this world keep fucking with our lives, whilst they are living a life of luxury. And they do, it's true. This is all thanks to you and me. It's our hard work, long hours, and piss poor wages that give them their honky-dory lifestyles.

I am so pissed off as a worker at the moment at the way Britain is run. I'll tell you what, if I could I would bugger off and live abroad. But even the chance of that is very slim, so I guess I'm stuck here. If you have a chance to escape, do so as quickly as you can; otherwise, if you don't, you watch out. They will have you in debt up to your eyeballs before you know it—if you're not already. One way or another, you must try and escape before it's too late.

I, for one, don't want to be in debt to anyone when I retire; and, may I add, I'm planning to retire at the age of 50, which is about ten years from now. Then that's me finished, mate! Oh yes—sir—ree! They can kiss my arse if they think I'm going to work longer than that. They can dream on. Those bastards have bled me dry long enough.

I hope you have the chance to do the same, but many of you will fall in the debt trap, if you haven't done so already. But look on the bright side—one thing you can bank on is this Government will give you plenty of time to pay it all off because, if they have their way, you will be working until you are 80. Well, you might as well be, because you won't qualify for a pension until then. And if you are still in debt by the time you do eventually retire—if you haven't snuffed it by then, that is—again, don't worry yourself about it too much, because they are setting up plans so you will be able to pass on the debt to your kids. After you die they can pay it all off for you. Don't even think your house will see to that, because there is a good chance you'll have to sell it to pay for you funeral.

Our so-called 'free' country, Great Britain, is getting better by the years. It is in debt, it's run on debt, and they live on the hope that we all stay in debt so that we keep working for peanuts until well into old age, as most of will do.

Let's hope the next generation of politicians see this flaw in our economics as I have pointed out, and pray that our future little politicians do better than these useless toss pots we have in now. Let's keep our fingers crossed they can turn things around. Mind you, even that future seems bleak now we have joined the European Union and if things continue we are all truly fucked. Frankly, I don't think people will bother voting anymore; we don't have any say in our own country's economics or future, anyway. I can see, before long, it will be all up to foreigners. The problem we face now is that these rich toss pots I talk of have got too bloody powerful for their own good and, if we continue to let them get away with it, they will continue to take over the world, and it'll be you and I who'll get caught up in the shit to come.

If I was in power I would make the minimum wage much higher and cap the earnings of big earners to, say, a maximum of two thousand pounds/dollars that any one person can earn in a week; everything above that would be confiscated and given to the health service, transport, education, etc. In fact, all health treatment would be free. If you voted for me, we wouldn't be in the dictatorship we have now, that's for sure.

This bunch of wankers we have in power do what they want and then it's us soft fuckers who keep paying for it. Like the war in Iraq—just that alone is still costing us a fortune. We didn't even want to go to war in the first place; it was just because two disillusioned religious fanatics thought they were doing God's work. It was to aid their plans for world domination. Blair and Bush were planning to take over the world. Now, there's a thought! HUM!!

That may not be as stupid as it sounds. I mean, when I come to think of it, it's obvious really. If they had control of all the oil of the world, they would in fact own the world. Bring back James Bond—there's a couple of loonies trying to take over the world! Besides, without the oil, how else was Bush going to hold on to the world record of the 'worst polluting country'? That medal can go on the shelf next to the trophy for the worst president America has ever known. In my opinion, he was.

MICKY FRICK'S TIP

NEVER BELIEVE A POLITICIAN—THEY ARE USUALLY FULL OF SHIT

When I take over the world, all overtime will be tax-free, I promise… because I am sick to the bollocks of the way we, the working-class people of Britain, keep getting constantly shit on, ripped-off and fucked by its very own elected government, when it seems they can't do enough for the immigrants coming in, can they? Bastards.

Here in the UK, every four years we have an election, when we have a choice between the Tories and New labour or, god help us, the fucking Lib/Dems, all shouting 'vote for me', yet they are all full of the same old bullshit. Who can we trust to lead this country for us? I don't know, do you? Tossers, the lot of them. What we all know is that, no matter who is in power, they will still tax us to high heaven, as they always do in one form or another; they will all continue to rip us off, lie, cheat, and deceive while, at the same time, they are filling their own pockets and filling our heads with all that eastern promise. Well, listen to me, wankers… Shut the fuck up!! We don't believe a word you say anymore. In fact, I think we are being run by a coalition government and they just aren't telling us. I think they have for years worked from one book of policies, and come polling day it's a public deception to make you think you have a say. It's like a game to them, and the winner gets Number 10. That's it, a trophy, that's all. It doesn't really mean shit to ordinary folk like you and I. The truth is, whoever wins the election works from the same book as before; it's all about winning the trophy, the keys to Number 10, and that's it. None of them have any significant different policies; they never have done. They just shuffle the ones they have and word them differently. They don't give a flying fuck about you and me.

It's always been the same, nothing has ever changed. Only these days, they are more interested in giving loads of our hard-earned taxpaying money away to fuckers who haven't even paid into the system and who are lining their own pockets. That pisses me off. And then they encourage even more sheep into this country who are prepared to work for peanuts, driving its own people out of work.

Do you know, I used to be proud of England. Now, I feel it's the arsehole of the planet, and is being pebble-dashed by asylum seekers and scroungers who abuse our hospitality and unknowingly fall into the pit in which we are all trapped. Britain is, officially, 'The Pitts'. Listen to me… if you're thinking of coming over here to work and live in England, don't fucking bother. We don't want you here. Most of the good people of Britain are pissed off with the place as it is; you're just adding to the shit. Besides, we really don't like you; we think you smell and are a bunch of fucking scroungers. By all means come and have a short holiday; we don't mind you coming over for a holiday, but after two weeks piss off back home, will ya? You'll be better off in the long run, trust me.

Living here is a dictatorship, too. You'll find that out in the end. We are all fucking depressed, just like you are. Money is worth fuck all here; the streets *aren't* paved with gold, believe me—just rubbish and used needles. Our dictators are just posh-talking, hairy-arsed wankers, who don't give a flying fuck about anybody but themselves. Count yourself lucky, my friend, because you can leave after a couple of weeks, but we can't. My message goes to you all: Don't come to England. It's a rip-off shithole. The government only allows you here because it wants to trap you and use you as cheap labour, or rip you off. Don't fall for it. Don't forget, it was us the British who used to have slaves (or 'volunteers', they like to call them these days).

MICKY FRICK'S TIP

NEVER VOLUNTEER. WHY SHOULD YOU WORK FOR FREE? ONLY DO VOLUNTARY WORK IF EVERYBODY YOU WORK FOR AND NEXT TO ARE DOING THE SAME. SOMETIMES VOLUNTEERING IS GOOD FOR THE SOUL, BUT LISTEN TO ME... IF SOMEBODY IS GETTING PAID AND YOU'RE NOT, THEN THAT'S WRONG. WHAT MAKES THEM SO SPECIAL?

Stress... I'll tell you about stress, shall I? I'm always stressed. It's watching brainwashed sheep like you lot that stresses me out, working for fuck all. Do you know, I wouldn't be so fucking stressed either if it wasn't for my colleagues at work. Have you noticed that when you're experiencing a stressed moment in your life, it is probably because another twat you work with has put you there in the first place? Every poxy day of my life some twat stresses me out, mainly one from work, because they are being a knob.

It's like the other day, I woke up one morning feeling okay, and then, as soon as I clocked in, a fucking smarmy twat says something to ruin my day. Or another time, I'd just woken up and, after a good fart, wash and a brush of the teeth, got dressed ready to face another event-filled day, when something had already started to stress me out; this was before I had even had my first cup of tea of the day. I made the fatal mistake of turning on my radio and found myself shouting at some thick twat talking about how he thinks workers should accept low pay to help companies out of the recession, or something along those lines. I got so wound up that I threw the fucking radio across the kitchen, spilling boiling water on my hand.

Okay, I am a bit ratty when I first wake up; I might have been just a little bit tired, and I don't really wake up until about two hours after getting out of bed, so that doesn't help, I suppose. I don't know about you, but I never have my full eight hours' sleep. They say you need to have about eight hours, don't they? Me, I probably only have about six, so there you go. I'm losing out on two hours sleep every day. With quick basic mathematics I learnt at school… I have worked it out. On a working week of five days, I lose ten hours sleep per week. That's like a lot of fucking hours. In fact, it's almost half a day every fucking week! No wonder I'm so tired all the time, and it's no wonder I'm looking like a walking zombie, and self-harming myself with boiling water. The only reason I'm up is because my alarm clock woke me up to go to work.

For the sake of interest, let's work this out—if there's 356 days a year, twenty-four hours per day, which is a total of 8,544 hours a year—minus my loss of sleep. Fucking hell, that bastard alarm clock is seeing me off about 520 hours' sleep every fucking year. Where's the hammer? Next Sunday, when my wife shouts 'IT'S TIME YOU GOT OUT OF BED!' I'll shout back 'FUCK OFF WOSHEEP, THIS BED OWES ME TEN FUCKING HOURS.'

MICKY FRICK'S TIP

GET PLENTY OF SLEEP

'When you dream your mind is defragging'

MAF

Interesting website on dreams to look at www.dreams.ca/

Do you know, anything can stress me out these days. A good one to start me off is seeing the washing-up in the kitchen sink overflowing. I wouldn't moan, but there are three people that live in our house, yet the sink is always overflowing and it's muggings here who usually has to do it. Work is stressful, from start to finish. It starts from when you set off and then when you come home. I find playing whale music in my in car stereo works a treat and, with a bit of luck, and if nobody has cut me up, I sometimes arrive at the shithole quite stress-free—but then you can guarantee some slimy bastard will say something to upset my whole day. Wankers. Why do we put ourselves through it?

You're An Insignificant sheep

As far as the government is concerned, you're simply looked upon as an insignificant sheep. The word 'insignificant' is defined in a dictionary as unimportant, irrelevant, not important, of no consequence, immaterial, inconsequential, not worth mentioning, and trivial.

Money is all the government focuses on. It doesn't care a toss about you as a sheep; you are just a commodity. As long as you're paying your way in the world, as long as you are bringing them in an income by working, paying taxes, spending your hard-earned money and what have you, you are totally insignificant to them.

No matter if you are filling shelves, cleaning toilets, a trades sheep or business sheep, as long as you're paying your dues they don't care a toss about you. The problem we have is that the sheep who run the world forget it is us, the working class of the world, who are the lifeline of everything that is. We are what make the world go round. Without us workers, basically nothing would get done, would it?

Yet, we the working class are treated as insignificant. We shouldn't have to fight for a pay rise, or practically beg for better working conditions; we should be worshiped. But no, we are treated like shit. We have to work overtime, or find another form of income to have any pocket money to buy nice stuff. All our wages are used up on taxes and bills, because working sheep are paid so poor we don't have any surplus money to buy anything nice for ourselves. The knock-on effect is that nothing needs to be made, so then jobs are lost, all because of rip-off companies such as insurance companies and banks.

If we, the working class, want something nice for ourselves we have to go into our overdraft or take out a loan; they are all screwing us, my friend. We are only in this recession because of the greedy, selfish corporate companies who are forever maximising their own profit though ripping us off, and then blatantly rubbing it back in our faces by awarding themselves with massive yearly bonuses, larger than some sheep will ever earn in a lifetime, especially banks. But do they spend it on stuff to feed it back into the system, which could generate work? Do they fuck. No, they are hoarding it in their own bank accounts. If they spend any, it isn't much. It's bastards like this who are running this planet. The banks run the world not the government, I reckon.

We need to kick-start production to get out of this recession. We need to re-generate the building trade and industry, get sheep working again, for good wages too. One thing is a fact—working sheep like to buy stuff. If stuff is affordable, they will buy it. The more they buy, the bigger the demand, which creates work. This is how everything ticks. And most of all, we must cap the earnings of these high earners and corporate company executives. If money isn't spent, it's just numbers on a computer and is worth nothing.

Now, changing the subject slightly, but did you know it has been said that Prince Charles (aka Big Ears), our future king here in the UK, has supposedly ninety insignificant sheep just like you and I as his servants? One apparently is employed to put his toothpaste on his toothbrush. So, I guess now he's married Camilla that will create another job for one more to load *her* toothbrush, too. Don't get me wrong, there is nothing wrong with being a servant; when you look at the unemployment situation in the UK, at least it's nice to know that ninety 'IPs' have work, created by our very own Prince. Because of him, they are earning a good wage for doing it, which is great. I mean, at least they are not sponging off the state, like some. Good for Charlie I say, if it's true. Why should I be concerned that Big Ears can't put his own toothpaste on his brush? I'm just pleased he's created a job for one of our fellow 'IPs'. Thank you, Charlie. And it gets me thinking, if the rich and wealthy sheep of the world could find meaningless tasks for unemployed sheep to do, we could generate loads of jobs. So, if anyone reading this is rich, don't hoard your wealth; give some sheep a job, say wiping your arse, but pay them well.

Just out of interest, does being called an insignificant sheep hurt your feelings? Well, face it, my friend—that's all you are. But, if some sheep asked you to wipe his arse and said he'd pay you £2000 for doing it, would you say no? Well, they say where's there's shit there's money. As an insignificant sheep, at least you know where we stand; you should accept the fact you are here to serve the rich, but at least we should be paid well for doing it. Like it or not, that's basically what we all do, anyway, it's just the wages are shit. I mean, when you think about it, that's all we mere sheep have ever done. Throughout history, we've been here merely to work our nuts/tits (don't want to sound sexist) off for the elite; so, saying that, why should we give a toss about anything else that goes on on this miserable planet?

It's not our fault—it's them, those upper-class tosspots. For years we have all been doing as we're told. We are not paid to think now, are we? We are paid to serve the rich. So fuck it, I say, and let's make the best of what life has dealt us. I'll continue just to be the monkey and, if they just keep paying me the peanuts as they do, I will shut the fuck up and dance the jig for them. And when everything goes tits up, I can say 'don't blame me'.

Yep, whether we like it or not, this is a fact of life; so no matter what we say or do, and no matter how much we protest about it, I don't think it matters much. We will continue to be ignored as we always have been. Our opinion isn't worth shit to them up at the top, and everything will continue as it always has done, generation after generation, until the world crumbles at the edges. Life for the worker has always been and will, forever, be shit.

MICKY FRICK'S TIP

DON'T TRUST BANKERS. THEY ARE WANKERS

So, I reckon if this is the case, as a worker you must try to do less work for your money. Fuck 'em. In your head, tell yourself what you think you're worth and work according to your imaginary hourly rate. Go to work and pretend you're on, say, twice as much as you're really on, in which case you would do half the work you normally do. Try and be more lazy than normal.

MICKY FRICK'S TIP

LEARN TO SKIVE

If you think about it, if you work half as much as you normally do, then only half the job will get done and the company will have to employ more sheep—50% more, in fact. That's the unemployment sorted out then, isn't it? Be less willing, less efficient—that's the key to bringing unemployment down, I reckon. Now, say you are given a contract of work that sets out what is expected of you; read it carefully, then play their rules back at them. For instance, only do what your contract expects you to do, no more; work at a slower pace, but—and this is *very* important—be a perfectionist at your job. Then, if the gaffer moans at you, tell him, 'you can't rush perfection'. And if you are tempted to climb the promotional ladder, I'll give you a tip: learn the art of bullshit.

MICKY FRICK'S TIP

LEARN THE ART OF BULLSHIT

Remember, even if you do get that promotion as a herder, you're still an insignificant sheep and you will still get shit on. So, all being said, you have to ask yourself, is the money and stress worth it? No, is the answer, if you think about it. Believe it or not, I was once a happy-go-lucky sort of sheep; nothing got me down, right up to when I was about fifteen, I'd say. At around that time I was just becoming a trainee, unsocialised rebel; I was footloose and fancy free and proud of it. Some sheep would say a delinquent. Whatever… But I must admit, little did I know then what life was really about and that life was going to give me a swift kick in the bollocks as I got older, and it did over and over again. You see, I was under this allusion that I had the world at my feet and that anything was possible; that I had the freedom to do whatever I wanted with my life and all that crap. You know the kind of thing I'm talking about; you're told this when you are just starting out in life at school. They really shouldn't fill our heads with so much shit.

Leaving school—which, for me, was in 1979—was the best day of my life ever (leaving school that is, not being at the shithole). I say best day of my life because, for about two hours after leaving, I felt proper free. In fact, as soon as I walked out of that lamb prison, I stripped off my uniform, set fire to it by the school gates, and walked home in my underwear. It was great.

It was only a day or so after when I suddenly realised I was not free at all; I had to get a job, which I was reminded of many times from my father. A job doing what? I didn't have a clue. I had no qualifications and the prospects of me ever getting a good job were poor, so this was the time when I started to come to terms with the fact that I'd probably have to do unskilled labour of some sorts, and my life looked bleak from there on. Year by year, bit by bit, I became more and more demoralised. Being new to this working lark and not knowing much about life, I still gave my all in everything I ever did and I worked hard. 'Adulthood sucks' was my thinking. They filled my head with false hope.

False Hope and Ambition

(A goal, hope, or ideal that is unlikely to be achieved or realised).

I have learnt, if you are not rich, you are most certainly under the allusion that, someday, you could be. Well, listen up, friend—you're living in false hope. This might be hard to accept, but you are never going to get wealthy enough to stop working, that's for sure. Well, 98% of you aren't, at least. There aren't many sheep in the world who will get rich enough to be able to stop working. Very few. In fact, those who do have money are either born into it or are crooks. And as for the 'American dream'—forget it. Any ambitions you may have are pointless; you may have dreams about working for yourself too, but don't bother. Waste of time. You may last two years, maybe three, but your government (the farmer) will not help your business grow. Not anymore, it won't.

Do you know, I was ambitious once. It's true! I was *very* ambitious, in fact. I wanted to be successful and rich and I worked damn hard to try and succeed at it, too. As you know, the motivation behind all ambitious sheep is usually money; they all dream of being their own boss and making millions. But this, also, can be a weakness. Once you get that bug, that ambitious streak, you tend to get selfish, over-tired, and boring, because you will soon find you will work even more hours than you did before, just to reach that unreachable target. And so you live, eat, and talk work. Every sheep will find you a boring twat. You'll start to neglect your family, you will walk over sheep, stab them in the back, all in your quest for this wealth.

Think about it for a moment—how many of you out there actually have your own business? Would you say you are loaded? You know—got plenty of 'maaaney'. What I mean to say is, would you consider yourself a rich sheep? 'No' is the answer to that, I'm betting. Not many of you said yes, that's for sure. I wouldn't be surprised if most of you are just about making a living, as we all are. This is because you are paying for stuff you have; and because of your wealth, you are just paying for more stuff. This is because sheep are naturally greedy. Ask yourself this: do you really need all that stuff? The big house, those expensive cars, et cetera, et cetera. The answer to that is also 'No'.

I bet if you was to calculate how much you earn each week to how much you spend against how many hours you've worked, you're not left with much left over, are you? I guess you just about meet all the payments on all the stuff you have. Ok, you may have a few quid to go out for a drink at the weekend, but that's about it. This is because you are suckered in thinking you need stuff, and think you are doing well because you have a lot of stuff, when really most of us work the extra hours just to pay for the stuff we don't really need. As a result, your health suffers and you're stressed out to the bollocks. So, to stop feeling stressed, you buy even more stuff you don't need and it goes on and on. Are you happy as a result? Like I said before, you're working your nuts/ tits off and just about earning a living, just because you all have stuff to pay for. We all live to our means, whatever your wealth.

You're not on your own, though. Every sheep, all over the world, that works for a living is doing the same. Why? Because of the brain-washing caused by advertising. If they didn't advertise you wouldn't know that product existed, and therefore you wouldn't want it or miss not having it. Simple. No matter where your money is coming from, at the end of the day you are just about earning a basic living to maintain your lifestyle. As I said, 'you live to your means'. The more money you have, the more you spend. Okay, so you may be driving a better car about than your neighbour, eating in posh restaurants, you may even have a large house. But I bet most of you haven't got much money left at the end of the week. It's all mainly down to the loans and overdrafts. Advertisements prey on greed. If you're doing so well, why then do you keep buying a lottery ticket? I'll tell you why—GREED.

MICKY FRICK'S TIP

DON'T TAKE OUT ANY LOANS UNLESS YOU HAVE ABSOLUTELY NO CHOICE. WAIT FOR THE THINGS YOU WANT. SAVE AND BUY IT IN CASH.

bloody advertising. Next they will be bringing out ram make up. Oh shit, they already have. We are fucked.

Can't you see? They are trying to get you to get in touch with your feminine side. And what's all *that* about? I'll tell you why that is; it's because ewes have always been deemed the weaker sex, and it is all to do with making *you* weak like a ewe (no offence, ewes). No wonder there are so many homosexuals in the world. I think they are just confused rams, unsure of their sexuality. It's because of this brainwashing, I reckon. It's all to do with this sheep-grooming that's taking off all around the world, all that designer perfume for rams. It's just not right.

There's nothing wrong with the smell of body odour—it's natural. Scientific tests have found that pheromones are in our body odour and have, for thousands of years, been used to attract the 'opposite sex'. If you don't like the smell of sweat, don't let your mate work so hard next to you; then they wouldn't smell so much, would they?

Body odour is natural. However, if it's coming from the same sex, it's natural to be repelled by same sex sweat. If body odour comes from some sheep who is the opposite sex to you, you wouldn't be bothered half as much—you may even be attracted to either sex. For me, being a real ram, the mere thought of a ewe's sexual bits turns me on.

My tip is this. If it's hot and you're sweating a lot, go and take a shower; wash with simple soap, and don't cover yourself with gay perfumes. Mind you, when I shower and use my wife's smelly shower gel, I get a hard on and usually have a wank. I do like that strawberry cream one… anyway, enough of that… Remember, it's all to do with these pheromones. A ewe is attracted to a ram's smell (sweat). Not dirty sweat, though that's minging. Watch out for the stuff they put in perfumes these days; they are all based on natural pheromones, but they are fucking about with them too much and now making them into unisex products, so no wonder we are all confused and the lesbian and homosexual population is for ever growing. Nobody is sure who they should be anymore; they are messing with our heads, dudes.

To stop myself turning gay, if a ram I meet smells nice I say to myself 'He's a homo. Watch your back. He wants to bum me.' Instantly I am on guard. Or, if he is too bloody close, I will face him square on and give him a mean stare. It seems to work for me, anyway. He soon fucks off.

Anyway, what are pheromones, I hear you ask?

(Pronounced 'FAIR-uh-moans') Pheromone definition: Pheromones are naturally occurring substances the fertile body excretes externally, conveying an airborne message to trigger a response from the opposite sex of the same species.

Pheromones were first defined in 1959 as chemical substances excreted by animals to trigger REPRODUCTIVE behavioural responses from recipients of the same species. Well, if they fuck about with it a bit, like they do, it could work on the same sex, too. Get my point? **B**ody **O**dour is your safe bet. Trust me. Keeps every gay sheep away.

Television

Another way of putting this idea into our heads is via TV advertisements. The television is a great tool for giving sheep false hope. It makes you think you stand a chance to, say, become famous or own a great big house, or a villa in Spain, or what have you. The more they show you on TV, the more you will believe it is possible. But the real goal is to keep you working, so always remember that. If you take any notice of it, you will start putting more hours in at work in your feeble attempt to make all your dreams come true when, in reality, it's never going to happen.

Have you noticed, as soon as you're flush one week from doing all that overtime, you can guarantee something will happen to make you spend the extra money you've just earnt on something completely different. You can guarantee something will happen to prevent you from buying whatever you were planning to buy or save for; for instance, an unexpected big bill will come through your letter box, or an appliance in your home will break and you'll need to replace it or get it fixed, or something along those lines. You never get the chance to reach that goal you have just worked your bollocks off to get. They are fucking with us sheep and it goes on and on and on all our sorry, fucking lives. It's all to do with keeping you at the level they want you at—which is a worker.

Television is used as a billboard to sell you false dreams. As you watch telly, subconsciously you think, 'I want that, I would love to have that. I need that, I could have one of them.' Well, let this be your big wake-up call, my friend. It will never happen— not whilst you are working class. Take it from me, if you're not born into money you're fucked.

The glitz and glam lifestyles like you see portrayed on the TV are only for the chosen few. Okay, I hold my hands up. I accept the odd few of you might get lucky, fingers crossed. But not many; and you will have to be very, very, *very* fucking lucky, too. But the majority of us will never have a taste of the good life. Of course, you knew that but chose to ignore it. Well, wake up my friend. Every sheep can dream, but that's all it is—a dream. Now, how frustrating is that? Excuse me while I kick the cat. And that's just a figure of speech, before my wife or you animal rights lot get all excited.

Someone once said to me 'There are sheep in this world who will amount to great things, and those that are merely to serve.'

Too fucking right. And not every sheep is wealthier than you, either, as is sometimes stated on TV. Sheep who have money very rarely watch TV, so it's aimed at the average Joe. You see, rich sheep can afford to go out and have a life. Sheep who watch TV usually are too skint to go out, or are already in debt up to their eyeballs. To many, sheep spend most of their lives watching TV. Well, you are daft fuckers really, aren't you? Life is depressing and bad enough as it is. TV is bad for your health, can't you see? They are just filling your minds with false hope. Turn the thing off. Stick a fucking hammer through it. You can watch TV when you retire and are too old and fucked to do anything else. Come to think of it… retirement. HA!! That's a laugh.

Retirement and debt

All through your working life you've probably paid into a pension scheme, trying to secure a nice retirement for yourself and your family, yet all your working life you are conditioned to want more stuff. This is what makes you willing to work for fuck all. But the fact is, you are forever chasing rainbows because they will never let you have that dream, namely a wealthy retirement. The more you make, the more the bastards will take. The good life and thoughts of having large amounts of money and blowing down the pub when you retire will never happen, not with these fuckers. How disillusioned you are if you think any different. You must realise that the more you work, the more you'll get fucked, and the more the taxsheep will take from you. Don't think about retirement; think about the now.

The more work you do, the more you'll miss out on life and time with your family. Enjoy nature, it's free. There are loads of good things you can enjoy that don't cost anything. Why wait for retirement, because by then you will be too fucked from working all your life and too old to do anything, anyway. Do you know, since I realised this, I haven't done half as much overtime as I used to, and I'm no worse off by it, either. I'm still surviving. I've even had time to write this book. Just goes to show, doesn't it?

What I'm saying is true. Deep down, you know this to be the case. So take my advice, live for today, and don't work so fucking hard. You'll be no better off from it. Can you imagine if all the working class of the world did that? It would be a much happier place, I think. This lust for material things soon becomes a drug, and a drug is something you don't need. As soon as you wake up and realise this, your life will improve. You work hard because you have been brainwashed to think you must.

MICKY FRICK'S TIP

DON'T LET YOURSELF GET INTO DEBT. IF YOU DO, THEY OWN YOU.

Do you have stuff, and a large stone of debt hanging around your neck at the moment? If you do, it's not your fault, really. You was brainwashed to spend money you didn't have. By getting you into debt they own you. Oh yes, sirree! They love you to get into debt. They know your weakness. They know you can't resist spending your money. They know you have to buy all the latest gear. They make you think you're a failure if you don't keep up with the latest stuff. They know you've got to have a better one than your neighbour—that better game console, the latest mobile phone. It goes on and on. You eventually end up in debt up to your eyeballs, and then they have GOT YA!

It's easy to get the working class into the debt trap. I mean, you're encouraged to get a new car; they do this by making the fucking MOT tougher for old cars. Have you noticed how much it costs to keep an old car on the road these days? You will guarantee it will fail the MOT on emissions. Ring any bells? There's fuck all wrong with your emissions, it's just a way of saying 'get into debt, buy a new car'.

We are under pressure to buy stuff. They control our thinking, putting these suggestions into our minds every chance they can. Buy this, buy that. The slimy bastards, they get you forever wanting for more, pushing you to work more hours to pay for it. 'The more you make, the more they take,' as I said. And before you know it, you then find yourself deeper in debt. Don't forget, you're only spending the bank's money—they will loan you as much as you want because of the interest they will rake in.

Robbing bastards. You have been brainwashed, you see, and they use the television, the radio or any other means possible to get you into that debt. They've got you where they want you. Once you're in that debt, and you're falling for it all the time, you feel you must buy something new just to bring happiness into your life. No you don't. Fuck 'em... You're all like moths to the flame; sheep are attracted to the idea of having stuff, then they get burnt. Stupid.

You have to take your hats off to them, though. I mean, it's working, isn't it? What a great master plan, to get every sheep into debt; they have a guarantee you'll work you tits off for peanuts to try and pay it all back and do all the overtime you can get. Your debt will appear to be decreasing very little because they can increase the interest on the borrowing, then you will be forced to work even harder to try and pay it off, or you'll have the fear of the bailiffs knocking at your door.

So, what I'm saying to you, as the voice of reason, is don't fall for it, my friend. Not anymore. Be strong, deny yourself until a later date when you can pay for it in cash. My advice is buy everything in cash. Listen to me, let's all start fucking them back or, better still, buy everything second-hand. Mind you, that's not such a good idea, come to think of it, because most of the things you buy new these days are of such poor quality that they'll be no good second-hand. That's how they get you to keep spending—they make stuff that's shit quality, then it won't last long and you will have to buy it again. Bastards.

I fucking don't like banks, either. They can't be trusted. We should never use a bank. Instead, save your money in your house; there are plenty of good safes you can buy these days. Antique ones, that is. At the moment, there are some still left, but until they start making them on the cheap you can still get new ones that will suffice. Keep your money in them and fuck the banks.

Also, you can get your own back on them by only buying what you really need. Always wait for a sale or barter with the seller to get the best deal. And for fuck's sake, never take out insurance or extended warranty for the stuff you buy, as it's pointless. They never pay out when you put in a claim in, anyway—or, if they do, it's a head ache.

MICKY FRICK'S TIP

DON'T TAKE OUT INSURANCE UNLESS YOU HAVE NO OTHER CHOICE. MOST OF THE INSURANCE COMPANIES ARE RELUCTANT TO PAY OUT IF YOU CLAIM ANYWAY. DO WHAT I DO AND BUY A SAFE. MARK IT WITH 'JUST IN CASE' AND PUT THE PREMIUMS YOU HAVE BEEN QUOTED IN THERE EVERY MONTH. IF YOU DON'T HAVE TO USE IT, IT'S A SAVING FOR OLD AGE, ISN'T IT?

What I do is ask how much the premium is, then put what they say as monthly payments in my own safe and save it myself. I call it my 'just in case tin'. I mean, how often do you actually claim on insurance, anyway? After a year, if you haven't needed it, open your tin and blow the lot down the pub. Fuck 'em. Bastards.

The shepherd will never let working-class sheep like you and me become rich. Who would do all the work if they did?

Who *would* do all the work, such as clean the toilets, sweep the streets, or look after the elderly? Nobody would. The rich think 'let somebody else do it'. That's why we have to have the rich, elite sheep who run your lives for you, and you will never, as long as you have a hole up your arse, be allowed to get as rich as them because 'who would do all the work'? Anyway, face it, we need to be told what to do. They know this—you're sheep, which means you can't manage yourself.

You've got to laugh. I mean, you could have it all. Everything could be oh so different, but you lot are too thick to realise what's going on. You'd rather accept this control instead of what could

ʋou are all so fucking gullible,
why we all live by a set of rules
g.... .. .. ʋy .... ɪarmers and shepherds of the world, because
we let them get away with it.

You can forget about retiring early, as well, as it will never happen. In fact, if you are lucky enough to live to reach retirement age, the way things are going your pension won't be worth fuck all, anyway. You really are stupid to think you will ever retire with plenty of money in the bank, so you can afford to do all those things you always dreamt of doing when you was working age. Unfortunately, you were born to work and there is every chance you will die working. So…

MICKY FRICK'S TIP

'DON'T WAIT FOR RETIREMENT. LIVE FOR TODAY'

Here is an interesting factoid.

Average life expectancy of Sheep—White Ram: 79 years; White Ewe: 87 years; Black Ram: 81 years; Black Ewe: 81 years.

So, if the farmer gets his way and you have to work until you're 75 before any pension is paid out, which has been considered, there is a very good chance you will die before you retire and never pick up any retirement fund at all. You will literally be worked to death. Remember, retirement age is 60 for ewes and 65 for rams at the moment; if they were to increase it, you will wear yourself out even sooner. If you're lucky you will have four, maybe even eight years of retirement in a nursing home, where the fuckers will use all your assets to pay for your care before you snuff it. Whoopee. Thanks for fuck all, you bastards.

The shepherds are watching you all the time; they have access to all your bank details; they know when you buy something with a visa or credit card; and if you buy a lot of stuff, they will assume you have too much money and find ways to take it from you. It's true. For example, when you get to retirement age they will find a way of taking your money from you then, too. So, all being said, it makes good sense not to keep your money in a bank at all.

My advice is this: take a leaf out of a pirate book and hide the lot somewhere other than a bank. Bury it in the garden under the slabs or something. But don't trust a bank… and this is very important too, so listen up. When you *do* decide where to hide your treasure (money), be sure you draw a good map showing the location, or buy an ordinance survey map and mark it with a big X and then hide the map; this is because, as you get older, your memory will not be as good as it is now, and it is likely you will forget where you buried your money, or even where you hid your map. So, give yourself a clue or a memorable word to remind you where the map is kept. That's very important. Make sure you put it in a place you—and only you—will know. Don't tell nobody where your map is hidden, and I *mean* nobody, except maybe your nearest and dearest I suppose, if you have to.

Here is a good idea where you could hide your map. Mainly, this is aimed at ewes. Statistics say that there is a very good chance that the ram in a relationship will die first, so maybe it would be a good idea to put your map behind a photo of your husband. And I'll tell you why us rams snuff it first, shall I? It's because of all the years of working our bollocks off to make ends meet, that's fucking why… Anyway, I can rant on some more later, but at the moment it's very important that we focus on where you hide your map and money. Now listen up, for fuck's sake. Don't tell any sheep your plan of what you're doing with your money, or your map come to that. Once all is done, it's very good practice to always plead poverty to family members and friends so they don't try and sponge off you while you're alive; they can have what's left when you snuff it, can't they? (By the way, this is very important as well—be sure you make a

'TRUST NOBODY FULLY'

Don't be proud. Accept any food parcels. Be grateful of any help. But—and this I must stress—remember, never ever trust the fucker!

Also, when you do get old, don't let any sheep get on your good side so you're tempted to leave them something in your will. They will only find a way to bump you off to get hold of the inheritance quicker. Times are hard, sheep do desperate thing in desperate times. So, I repeat, don't trust any fucker. I know, I know, I sound a bit of a miserable fucker, full of the joys of spring and all that. Well… that's because I am a miserable fucker. And when I get old, I will probably be a miserable old git.

Look, my friend, I know it seems a lot of effort to draw maps and hide your money and that. In fact, the best thing to do really is spend the lot whilst you're young enough to enjoy it. But on the same note, money doesn't always bring happiness, especially when you're getting on in years. When you're old, your health is your wealth, but health care can cost a fortune, too, and why should you pay out all your savings to be looked after when you get old? You've paid into the system all your life. Here in Britain, our muttons are treated like shit, unless you can pay for it, that is… It's not right, is it? Loneliness is also a sad factor.

As you get older, you may get lonely. Loneliness is something most old sheep experience once their spouse has died. You can, if you prefer, find friends by going to a retired sheep club, or joining some sort of organisation; but that's boring, I think, and it costs money, too. So, the best option is to break the law. That's right—break the law. Don't do anything too bad, of course. I'm talking along the lines of shoplifting that way, you only get sent to prison for a short time.

Now, the best time to break the law is when you're not feeling to well, or say you need a new hip replacement or something; that way, once you are inside His Majesty's pleasure, they are obliged to look after you whilst inside, so it'll be like a short holiday where they fix you up, feed you well and it's costing you nothing. It'll give you a bit of company for a while, too; a place where you can chat to interesting sheep instead of listening to some old fucker moaning about their aches and pains down the club. But, again, don't trust any inmates, either; you're in prison, remember, and they are mainly scumbags, but interesting ones, I would think...

If prison isn't an option for you, I suppose you can go and join that tea party or club of some sorts, whatever floats your boat. But, for fuck's sake, never use home help supplied by the local government—it'll cost you a bomb.

I recommend paying a friend or family member to look after you when you're old. But on the same note, don't pester your family too much; as far as they're concerned, they don't mind helping you a little but, to be honest, they would just prefer you to die than become a burden. Life is for the young, remember. When you're old, they don't want to be bothered. They'll just put you in a home in the end, then you'll really be up the swanny. You'll want to die just to get out of there. To be fair, when you get old you're just a fucking nuisance—you are, it's true, and you know it. To be honest, you'll probably smell of piss, and nobody likes an old smelly fucker; you won't attract any sheep smelling of piss. You're no use to any sheep if you're honest. When you're old, death is the best option. God knows that, and that's why old sheep die. It's the order of things.

So saying all that, you must make plans to look after yourself. And when you are in your later years, the message is this: fuck

... contribute to society
any...... you should just hurry up and die, although they'll never admit to it. They know the world's over-populated as it is—'out with the old, in with the new'. Besides, if you're left to be looked after, it's going to cost the economy too much money to keep you alive, and you'll only get in the way considering the fast pace the world is moving—driving slow and walking slow, you know what I mean. It all costs money and a government-run old sheep's home costs money, too; so, if you can't pay for it, and *they* have to, they will most probably put you in the most crappy old sheep home they can find, and then they speed up the dying process by turning up all the central heating to full whilst feeding you uneatable toxic waste that they got on the cheap. And to help hurry things along even further, they'll also pump all those drugs into your body without you knowing.

It seems to me they want you to have a crap old age. Why do you think the old age pension is so crap and most old sheep have a raw deal by the NHS? Because you're not worth saving anymore, that's why. You don't work; you don't contribute; they are trying to kill you off. You've outlived your use, you oldie. Commence the sheep culling programme... Yet, on the other hand, if they know you have money, they'll get you in the most expensive home they can find, they'll treat you like a king or queen; but they will seize all your assets to pay for it, so you will be left penniless anyway. Then, when your money has run out, they'll bump you off.

I know it all sounds horrible, but I'm just trying to make you understand you must plan to look after yourself, because when you get old nobody else will. I worry too much, like most sheep of today. I really do. You think you old fuckers have got it bad, well I think life's even harder for young sheep today. There is no work and every sheep is turning into a nasty bastard because of it, including me. We have been conditioned all our lives to be workers. We are brainwashed into thinking we must work. Yet, there are no jobs these days, there aren't even any unskilled labour jobs. The only jobs you'll find, if you're lucky, are shit computer jobs, like call centre jobs, that pay piss poor wages.

To make matters worse, the youth of today aren't coping too well, hence the drug culture. This is because the need for material things is rammed down their throats; they expect everything to be available to them. It's not their fault, granted. In this get rich quick commercial world we live in, sheep have become too demanding and don't understand why they can't have what they want when they want it. It's almost like they expect to be able to have what they want, when they want it; if not, they will steal it. Hence the riots of Britain in 2010, for instance.

MICKY FRICK'S TIP

DON'T LET CALL CENTRES GET YOU DOWN. THEY ARE ONLY TRYING TO DO A JOB.

Do you know, I'd be a lot happier if I kept away from other sheep and I could just disappear somewhere. In fact, I may one day just do that—disappear into the mountains where I couldn't be found, where there is no News, no TV, no radio, and no way of knowing what's happening in this fucked-up world, like that Grizzly Adams bloke. I could grow my own food, go hunting for fresh grass… fuck it, I'd eat insects. Basically, I'd live off the land, shit in the bushes, swim in the lakes, baaaa… It must be nice to be really wild and free like a mouflon (wild sheep), out of the clutches of other programmed sheep. Just me, living in the wilderness, until I'm an old piece of mutton; then, when I know it's my time to die, I will just dig a hole, bury my head in that hole so my arse is sticking in the air, and I will then have a pre-made tombstone alongside me saying 'You can kiss my arse'. Ha ha ha… In fact, show me those hills, I'm coming now! Beats working.

MICKY FRICK'S TIP

DON'T WORRY IF PEOPLE DON'T LIKE YOU, JUST TAKE PITY ON THEM AS THEY ARE MISSING YOUR FRIENDSHIP AND AVOID THE FUCKERS

CHAPTER TWO

MIDLIFE CRISIS

My midlife crisis was a direct result of the realisation I have done fuck all with my life because of being programmed to work. I missed most of it because I was too busy being at work. It isn't until that first back ache you realise 'fuck me, I'm getting old'.

2 April 2008

The Signs

When do you know you're hitting your midlife crisis? Well, it's usually when you start to ask the question 'What have I done with my life?' Then you know you have just hit it. I think, if the question 'When do you think you will hit your midlife crisis?' was put to sheep in the field, my guess is they would probably say it's about the age of fifty. However, I disagree. I think it's more like thirty—it was for me, anyway. I mean, look what happens to you by the time you hit thirty. At thirty, most of us have been holding a steady job for some time, if we're lucky, and there's a good chance you have an ongoing mortgage; with any luck, you're still married or, if not married, at least in a long-term relationship, and there is a good chance you both have lambs.

Maybe you've never been married. Well, if you *are* one of those who have never been married and are still single, you are probably starting to feel that, if you don't get a move on soon, you're going to be left on the shelf. Do you know what's really scary about a midlife crisis? It all happens without us even realising –one day, right out of the blue, you realise you're getting old. Of course, nobody will admit to it—we attempt to deny it, ignore it. Well, after all, there's bugger all we can do about it, unless you pay loads of money to hide it through cosmetic surgery. Failing that, what do we do? We try and disguise it in other ways, like buying sports cars, dressing in young modern cloths, Adidas sportswear—which, to be honest, looks out of place on a fat, middle-aged bastard like you. Yep, we do whatever we can to hide the fact we are getting old. But, no matter what you try and do, you can't turn back the clock and, as they say, 'If only I knew then what I know now.' By then, it's too late.

I'm now getting on a bit and just coming to terms with the fact I'm getting 'past my sell by date'—physically, but not mentally, may I add—and I have accepted the fact I am probably doomed to work for the rest of my sorry life. I know I don't look cool or trendy anymore; in fact, I look a complete dickhead with my shirt tucked into my jeans with the top button open, showing off my medallion I bought on E-bay, and a complete pervert when I go to nightclubs. The young girls I fancy only see me as an old fart or are worried in case I'm their mate's dad looking for them. Basically, I shouldn't even be there to be honest; I look like a paedophile at best, and dad-dancing is so un-cool. Not only that, I now realise I have wasted half of my life trying to make something of my life, and by doing so I feel I've missed out on a lot of things. Now that I'm better off money-wise than I have ever been before, I'm too old to do anything with it. So I go out and buy a motorbike. Now I'm a fat biker—how un-cool is that?

MICKY FRICK'S TIP

'NEVER PUT YOURSELF DOWN'

I don't know, you get fucked at school, they fuck you at work, we are always and will forever be fucked, and at the end of it you're physically fucked. And the only enjoyment you get out of life, at the end of the day, as a ram, is hoping some young dolly bird at a nightclub wants to fuck you. Then you remember you're a married sheep and don't really want to have sex with a dolly bird; you just want to be fancied by her, as that will suffice.

Tell you what, I'm going to look on the positive for a moment. Let's look into what can be considered as good. At the moment, I for one still have all my wool… that's good… even though it is starting to turn grey-ish, it just makes me look distinguished… that's good… My health isn't bad… that's good… and I have all my teeth, that's also good. So, all's good really. Now, let's look at whether my life has been good… So, what have I done with my life? Not a lot… that's bad… that didn't last long, did it? In fact, life has got me so wound-up I decided to write about it. I think I have missed most of my life by caring too much about shit, that's bad… Bollocks, I'm not only old… I'm a grumpy old git.

MICKY FRICK'S TIP

GROW OLD GRACEFULLY AND MATURE LIKE A FINE WINE

I remember once I walked out of my job in a strop. I was at the end of my tether with all the shit and, as a result, I was off work for almost four months. I'd just had enough, to be honest, and I was totally stressed. I walked up to the gaffer and said 'See you Easter', and coolly walked out the building and went home. It felt great at the time. Mind you, I was lucky I didn't get sent to the slaughter house or something. That would have been bad… but I didn't, gladly. But saying that, maybe if I had it would have done me a favour. I've now worked for the same company for twenty years and I'm still there… I wonder what I would be doing now if I had been released? I don't know, probably being fucked by some other employer.

You know, there comes a time in your life when drastic measures are called for. I was so pissed off I was prepared to give up working and never go back again. I nearly went to the mountains, but if I'd done that how would I have supported my family, or pay the mortgage and the bills and what have you? See, there I go again, a sudden fucking reminder of the fact that I'm a slave and I have to conform. You can't escape it, can you? Getting released would of done me a favour. I could of packed in working all together and claimed off the state—mind you, I would probably have got very bored.

Ten years later, I'm no longer stressed. Instead, I'm depressed. Great… I think I was heading to this midlife crisis the moment I left school, to tell you the truth. It was when I started working life, in fact on that bastard Youth Training Scheme—or YTS—that bright idea the Conservatives came up with back in the 80s, getting you to work for a minimal wage of £25. They should try and live on a measly £25 a week—£15 board and lodgings and £5 train fare to college. And if I wasn't at college, I'd have to work for 8 hours on a stinking building site in all weathers. MPs are really fucking wankers, aren't they?

MICKY FRICK'S TIP

DON'T LIVE IN THE PAST

Since that youth training scheme, I have been slowly heading towards this midlife crisis of mine, I reckon, because every job I've had after that day paid piss poor wages. Because of that YTS, the bastards who employed me knew I'd work for peanuts. I never had a chance to get on my feet after that. Come to think of it, maybe it's not a midlife crisis at all—but a realisation? I finally have realised I am never going to be allowed to earn proper money or make anything of my life. No wonder I've turned into the moaning old bastard that I am today. No wonder there are so many miserable bastards in the world. I'm not on my own! It's a realisation that we all have been taken for fools all our lives.

All this stress has been manifesting in us all—incubating itself within us over the years like a bad virus. Our experiences of life, the back-stabbing sheep we have met, or the hard work over the years, all the badly-paid jobs we've had to do at some time, and all those long hours we've all had to work have taken their toll in this pointless attempt to scrape a living together. We're just trying to have a half good life while having loans to pay back and ever increasing bills forced upon us, not forgetting putting up with all them shit gaffers we've all worked for at one time or another.

What with the constant lies from our leaders, and the propaganda and bad news we hear on the news—it has put us all in a spiral of hate, jealousy, greed, and frustration. No wonder the country's falling apart… What the fuck can we do about it? I tend to think life is such a disappointment, as our heads are constantly filled with false hope, like winning the lottery for instance. I wonder sometimes if there is a purpose to life at all.

MICKY FRICK'S TIP

NEVER READ NEWSPAPERS. READ FUNNY STUFF

Maybe we should ask ourselves searching questions like 'Have we even got a purpose?' I ask this because everything I have ever done in my life seems to have been a waste of time. I have given my all. Fuck knows, I have tried whole-heartedly to make something of my life. I should have continued claiming benefits all my life, like the other scumbags out there; but no, I didn't, and what thanks have I ever received for all my efforts? Fuck all. What, I ask you, have I got for contributing to the system all my life? I'm forever trying, but I don't seem to be getting anywhere; it's like pissing in the wind. I think I've had more of my fair share of disappointments, thank you very much. Well, sod it. I give up.

Do you know what gnaws at me the most? I've started to hear my teacher's voice in my head saying, 'Boy, you will never amount to anything', and 'You're a waste of space'. Perhaps the fucker was right, after all? I *am* a waste of space. At school, all I ever wanted to do was have fun. No harm in that, you would have thought. What's wrong in having fun, I ask you? I *was* a kid, after all. When I failed at school, the only encouraging comment from any sheep was from my mother. She said to me 'Don't worry, you're just a slow developer.'

Was trying to be a lamb such a crime? Was it wrong to hold on to my childhood and have fun? My brothers constantly reminded me that I was thick, as both of them was a lot cleverer than me a school. Maybe I *was* thick. I guess I still am. All I can say is 'Oh well, fuck it then'. If that's so, then I can't be blamed for anything I do, can I? I know I'm not the cleverest bloke in the world—don't want to be. You have got to laugh, though. I remember my mom telling me, 'Not every sheep can be a brain box, but it doesn't mean you can't be successful in other ways', then she would follow that statement with something like 'Anyway, Winston Churchill couldn't spell'. And I would ask, 'Who the fuck is Winston Churchill?'

Oh, and not forgetting this good one: 'If you want something bad enough, son, you have to work for it'. That's what my Dad said. Fucking hell, what a load of bollocks that was. Sorry Dad, but it's true. The funny thing is, it seems I was thick enough to believe the shit I was being told at the time. I understand now that my Dad was just programmed to programme me. It wasn't his fault, I see that now. Remember, programmed parents programme you. Well, I'm older now and a little wiser, I hope.

It's a fact that most things you're told are all crap, especially being told you can be successful if you work hard—that's the biggest load of bollocks for a start. I'll tell you what, it's all about luck at the end of the day. I get annoyed at statements like 'You must work hard to achieve your goal' that are fed to you from a young age to make you think that you, too, could be successful by working hard. It's all about getting you into the working rat race. They are brainwashing you into making you feel you *want* to work, feeding you on false hope—that's what I think, anyway. Remember, your parents are programmed to programme you, as I said earlier, so you can't blame them for your failed life. They know no better.

MICKY FRICK'S TIP

NEVER TAKE ADVICE FROM ANYBODY WHO HASN'T ACHIEVED ANYTHING IN THEIR OWN LIFE

Here is a word of advice. Never take advice from some sheep that has never achieved anything in his or her life. Now, that's good advice, so remember it.

Ever since this midlife crisis of mine started, there have been a lot of issues going on in my mind that never used to bother me before, but do now. One of my pet hates is political correctness. I really don't like those politically-correct knobheads who go on ranting on and dictating to us to what is right and wrong, when it is *they* who are wrong. And we must all be careful not to offend any sheep that are black. Don't those politically-correct sheep just irritate you? They do me; in fact, it would be safe to say they really piss me off, especially when they talk about the black community—sorry, the 'ethnic minority'.

Whilst I'm on the subject, fancy banning the nursery rhyme 'Baa baa black sheep' in schools! And why start calling the 'black board' a 'chalk board' for fuck's sake... It was in 1971 that the 'Golly' was banned form Robinson's jars, because of the fear it would offend black sheep. How pathetic is that? In fact, the year 1971 was the start of all this political correctness fiasco. Come on!! How the fuck can a cartoon picture of a little black sheep with curly wool upset any other black sheep? I have a lot of black friends from all 'ethnic backgrounds' and I reckon, if I showed them a picture of the 'Golly' and asked them whether it offended them, my guess is not one of them would say 'yes'. Why? BECAUSE IT'S A FUCKING CARTOON!

In my opinion, it is this fucking 'political correct brigade' that cause all the racist problems of the world, especially in this country. They dig up a problem that doesn't exist and then plant the idea that it's wrong in the heads of sheep, and the other sheep follow. Oy! Politically-correct knobheads—get a life! You need your heads held under the sheep dip for a while. Baaa!

I'm in a mid-life crisis and I'll tell you what I'm going to do. I'm going to buy a black BMW and play rap music as loud as I can. I'm going to have my wool dyed black and have an afro perm. Fuck it. I'm going to shout out loud, 'Power to the sheep!'

MICKY FRICK'S TIP

ALWAYS GO AND VOTE BUT ALWAYS SPOIL YOUR VOTING SLIP. I USUALLY PUT 'NONE OF THE ABOVE'. WELL, IT MAKES ME HAPPY

Do you vote? Unlike most of the population, I have always voted and I will always go and use my vote, come rain, sleet and snow, hell or high water; even if I have to crawl on my belly through shit, I will make damn sure I get down that polling station and make my mark come polling day. Oh yes indeed, my friend, that you can be sure of. It's not as if I don't have better things to do; far from it, there are loads of other things I could be doing, but you can guarantee I will make my traditional mark.

Don't get me wrong, I know all politicians (shepherds) are the same. They are all, in my opinion, useless two-faced lying wankers, all of them. A total waste of a space in my opinion, but it does give me the personal satisfaction just to go down that polling station armed with my 'black' marker pen (notice I said 'black' marker pen, not an ethnic marker pen. That's because that's what it is—A BLACK FUCKING MARKER PEN) and put a whacking great big cross across the lot with the words 'NONE OF THE ABOVE'. That so does satisfy me. I call unto you all reading this book to go out and do the same. Let the wankers know how you feel about them.

By the way, if you take offence at me saying a black pen being called a black pen, you may notice this book is also written in black ink and the book is black and white. If you find this offensive, go and fuck yourself, you knobhead. Who said you can read my fucking book, anyway? Do you know, joking apart, in this mad world of ours it wouldn't surprise me if somebody *will* be offended?

'I'm free from all prejudices. I hate everyone equally'

WC FIELDS

For me, as like WC Fields, I hate more a less everyone, so I'm neutral across the board. Except those who have bought my book, that is… I love you x

Whilst I'm on the subject about the political correctness brigade, let me speak on behalf of the white sheep of the world—I don't like school blackboards being called a whiteboard or chalkboard. I find if totally offensive. I don't care a flying fuck what other colour names you want to call me—I'm white and proud. You can call me spook, pale face, chalky, white bastard even. Call me what you want, I don't find it offensive at all. Even if it comes from a black sheep. Black sheep are too sensitive, I reckon.

Ask yourself this… when was the last time you heard a white sheep complain over a black sheep calling him names because of him being white? NEVER!! And it's not because black sheep aren't saying it—they are, but white sheep don't give a fuck, generally.

So, the black sheep don't bother calling us names very often. Instead, they get to us know by jumping on the bandwagon and making out they are the persecuted minority all the time. I must add, not all black sheep make a big deal of name-calling, but the ones who do, in my observation, are usually the ones who make something out of it; they make a big song and dance for their own gain. If there is something they can gain by accusing some sheep of being a racist for some remark, they will use their colour to get it, even if they don't really care at all.

Factoid:
A study taken in 2008 showed that white American sheep believe they are more discriminated against than black sheep these days:

> http://www.dailymail.co.uk/news/article-1390205/
> Whites-suffer-racism-blacks-Study-shows-white-sheep-
> believe-discriminated-against.html#ixzz24nDL5NsD

Every sheep is racist in one form or another, at some time in their life. And so what? What's the big deal, really, at the end of the day? We are all just sheep, are we not? Most of it usually manifests itself as a verbal insult towards some sheep behind the wheel of a car when some sheep has just cut you up; or in the company of you and your friends or family when you are watching a game of football on the TV; or sometimes it can get overheard by someone passing by and have found your comments offensive. If that happens, and you realise you have offended that sheep, you should apologise to them and the matter should be dropped there and then. Mind you, if every sheep were to just ignore insults or remarks that were said in the heat of the moment and which weren't directed at them personally, there wouldn't be a problem anyway.

MICKY FRICK'S TIP

NEVER BE TOO PROUD TO APOLOGISE

I believe that protests by Neo Nazis, or Anti-White Hate Groups, should all be banned, especially if they have an agenda that winds some sheep up. That just makes simple sense to me. Any sheep that preaches the hatred of one's race, or has a religious agenda that disrespects other sheep's views, is wrong. It's this kind of disrespect that shouldn't be allowed. And no, it's not freedom of speech. Freedom of speech is having the freedom to speak what you're thinking, as long as it isn't offensive to others. However, slagging off the shepherds and the farmer is different. I say different because their actions offend every sheep, no matter what their colour or religious persuasion. I find it offensive because they treat most of us with utter contempt. If it weren't for these fucking cretins, maybe there wouldn't be so many wars or innocent sheep dying needlessly across the world, would there? Think about it.

Freedom of speech—does anybody really have it? I'm not so sure. It's funny how we think we have freedom of speech until you want to use it—yeah, you have as long as you don't say or do anything the shepherds don't like. I think we are almost living under a dictatorship, because lately it seems the sheep of Britain have no say in what happens in this country at all. Like joining the European Union. If we had freedom of speech, or any say at all, we would have been given a referendum. Why didn't we have one? I'll tell you why—because the sheep would have said 'No'. We knew it would go tits up from the start and, sadly, we have been proven right. They, the shepherds, also knew it would go tits up. But I tell you this—the farmers of the EU also knew it would go tits up, but could also see there was a lot of money to be made as a result, for their own personal gain, not you and me. Farmers of the governing world are corrupt. They couldn't give a flying fuck about the sheep, mark my words.

A Dictatorship

The term 'dictatorship' refers to the way a leader gains and holds power, not the watch kept on the citizens. Some dictators, because of their popularity, have not had to employ many oppressive measures. The term generally has a pejorative meaning in reference to a government that does not allow a nation to determine its own political direction by popular election. Do you still think you're not in a dictatorship? If you think we are not, then, if you ask me, that's really fucking scary and just goes to show how good the farmer arseholes are in using their shepherds to brainwash you. It's simply further evidence that we are all turning into programmed conformist sheep. We are now living in a nanny state. The world is in a recession and we are constantly being told we are in it together. No, we fucking are not. The only sheep affected by this recession are the working sheep—that's me and you.

Can you tell me why the farmers and certain front bench shepherds are still living it up in their lavish lifestyles, along with their wealthy sponsors, when we still have increasing poverty and suffering in the world? Can you tell me why these fuckers get away with it? It's because most of those shepherds with good intentions are blind to what's really going on. This fear of 'you can't do that, you can't say this' bollocks is making you frightened to speak up. They say it's 'un-politically correct' to say that. You are not allowed to speak against political decisions and the vote you take in elections mean 'diddly squat', because they all sing from the same hymn sheet when you really think about it. Surely, that's bordering on a dictatorship, isn't it? You may well be thinking, 'Well, what if we are? There is nothing we can do about it'. Well, you would be very wrong indeed, as we can do a lot. Okay, they may well be winning at the moment, but they haven't beaten us yet.

Don't forget, we still have sheep power. We can stop all this shit. With the use of sheep power, we could form, say, a coalition union for sheep; you pick a group of working-class sheep, chosen by us to represent us, from every industry of the world—'The knights of the round table', if you like—who would stand as spokes rams/ewes for us all. They would bring to the attention of the useless shepherds the fact that the sheep of the world have had enough. If organised right, we would then have the power to hold the world to ransom; we could begin to set out our demands by telling them fuckers at the top exactly what's pissing us all off. Our representative could make a list— that we all help with, of course—and then hand it to whoever on our behalf. We would say 'Meet the workers' demands by improving their working lives, or else reap the consequences, you tosser…' or words to that effect. We would do this on New Year's Day, right at the beginning of a new year, so the next year we would have something to look forward to.

Here is a quick draft letter to Britain's farmer to give you an idea what should be put in the letter. The rest of the world could do the same. See what you think:

M. A. FRICKER

To the Governing body of the British sheep
10 Downing Street
London. Near Big Ben

Dear Head Farmer, PM
    By order of the sheep coalition, we hereby give you,
the head farmer of this country, a deadline of one year
to comply with all our demands listed below. If, by this
time, these demands are not met, we will refuse to go into
work each Monday until you bloody well do as we ask.
Listed below are the things we want.

Work.
    A fair day's pay for a fair day's work. For instance,
we want a minimum hourly rate of twenty pounds an
hour, not the fucking pittance it is now.
    We want the introduction of tax-free overtime.
    We want one week's holiday for every four weeks
worked with full pay, plus paid holiday leave on our
Birthdays.
    Health.
    We would like to see a totally free, first-class health
service, better than BUPA, available for all sheep who
hold a full-time job (if any sheep has to wait for treatment
longer than a week they will get compensated to the sum of
one thousand pounds for every day they go over this time).
    Dentist care, eye care, etc—including spectacles—
should all be free to those who work.
    Sheep who do heavy lifting or what would be classed
as hard work get a free masseur by a sexy model to ease
their aches and pains once a week if required.
    Ewes should have five years off with full pay when
she has a lamb. The husband can have ten weeks off in
the first year of the birth until the child is one year old
and becomes a sheep.

Entertainment

    Working sheep shouldn't have to pay for Sky TV. In fact, all TV entertainment should be free to working sheep. We want you to do away with the TV licence completely, and all telephone calls should be free to 'workers', and we want to have discounts on cinema tickets or theatre tickets, etc, because we work.

Education

    Our lambs are the future, so start thinking of our lambs for once. We want you to bring back proper apprenticeships for our lambs, so we don't have to employ any more foreigners to do the jobs. For those lambs who wish to stay on to further their education, we require that all further education should be totally free. We, as parents, expect a university standard education for all our lambs, irrespective of the child's ability. All lambs should have a fair chance to better themselves.

Welfare of this Country

    We want to see fewer coppers on the streets, and harder sentences carried out for scumbags.

    We want to see our country's industry flourish like it once did before you fucked it up. Stop selling off all our industry.

    We want to see more of our own produce being made and grown.

    We want to be self-efficient. Fuck the world—we want to see our farms growing our own food, producing our own meat.

    We want all basic amenities like Gas, Electric, and Water to be funded by you. We expect it to be top quality all the time, and cheap or even free, and available to all British nationals. We want our fuel costs halved to fall in line with the rest of the world. Stop ripping us off with petrol charges. It's wrong. Companies should not be allowed to boast of massive profits made—we say give some of that success back to the British sheep, use it to fund all aforementioned and start charging foreigners for using our roads.

Retirement

Old sheep have a raw deal. They should be treated better than they are, and respected more. We think it's only fair to offer sheep the chance of early retirement at the age of, say, 50. We think when a British worker reaches the age of 50, they should have the choice to stop working if they want to. If they do decide to stop working, they should receive a retirement gift—a 'thank you' if you like, for all their years of contributing to society. You, the farmer, should give them £50,000 for services rendered so they can enjoy the rest of their lives whilst they are still young enough to do so.

You may ask, all well and good, but how do we pay for all this? Well, it's easy. Get the money off them who boast about the massive profits they make, or those fuckers like yourself who have millions, if not billions, of pounds hidden away. Get the money from the twats who have been ripping us off all these years. Get the money from the ones who have it sitting in a bank somewhere, doing fuck all, when it could be put to better use and spent on the workers, industry, the health service, pensions, the security of this country, and our lambs' education. Eat that, you bunch of bastards and Happy New Year.

Yours sincerely,

THE COALITION UNION OF THE WORKING
CLASS OF GREAT BRITAIN

Okay, a little far-fetched, granted, but you get my point. The thing is, we have the power to change our lives for the better if we could be bothered to do so. But we don't seem to be bothered. It's important to pick the right sheep to do the job of running this country for us; some sheep who cares and knows what they are doing. Now, that would be a real bonus if we had both, unlike the fuckers we have now who don't have a clue. Maybe they do, but don't seem bothered either.

MICKY FRICK'S TIP

COMPLAIN MORE

If you ask me, we don't moan enough in Britain. We should be more like the French sheep, I say. We don't stand up for our rights like they do. We are supposed to have the freedom of speech in this country, so we should all use it more than we do. Sheep have the power to change the way things are. Power to the sheep!! But I guess you can't be bothered.

I was once thinking of standing for an independent party in the next general election, but that costs a lot of money and I'm 'skint' at the moment. However, if I was to miraculously come into some money, then I might still do so, and by Christ there would be some changes—a lot of changes, believe you me.

I don't know about you hard-working sheep of our once great nation, but I think this bunch of twats we have in power today have no interest in you and me. When they tell us they need to put up taxes, I have this burning urge to kick the Chancellor in the nuts. No wonder we all take out a loan –it's because of those robbing bastards. We don't have any of our own money left. The country itself is billions of pounds in debt, yet this government still feels it's okay to force us to take out a loan. No matter what you may think, you are not in control of your own life. You see, you forfeited that privilege because sheep are naturally very lazy fuckers and, besides that, we don't have any backbone to stand up for ourselves. If we are told to do something, even if we don't want to do it, we would still do it. That's why we have, and always have had, a bunch of toss pot directives that give us orders because we haven't got the bollocks to say 'get fucked'. So, I guess we kind of deserve everything we get. If you're not going to challenge the wankers, then you have no right to moan about the crap they dish out. Society gets what society wants at the end of the day.

That's our problem—we just let them get away with anything they want to. We know our lives are crap mainly because of them, but we accept it. It's true. Very rarely do we ever revolt, stand up and protest about something we don't like (Conformists, the lot of you). We do have our moments but, even on those very rare occasions when we do have a moan, it isn't long before we are all back to doing as we are told again, as before.

It always has been a mystery to me why we don't stick it out to the dreaded end. Why start a fight if you're not going to finish it off? That's the problem with us working-class sheep. When the directive shouts 'shit!' we jump on the shovel. You're all wimps, if you ask me. Now, because all the heroes are gone, our unions grow weak and our will to fight back is diminished thanks to years of Maggie Thatcher. Oh yes, you was beaten back by a ewe. YOU POOFS. Bloody hell, remember Old Maggie? That ewe was more like a cow, she destroyed our will to fight back in the 80s by deciding to close the pits. You should be ashamed of yourselves—I thought pit sheep were supposed to be tough and you was beaten by a ewe…

Actually, come to think of it, it wasn't *all* her fault; I don't suppose I can blame her solely. It was a mixture of her and the rest of the political know-alls. Systematically they sold everything that was once British, and the foreigners lapped it up. We tried on occasions to save everything that was great about Great Britain, but failed miserably as, at the same time, these tossers were selling us down the river; they destroyed the unions' power and the rights of the worker. We was put back almost to the dark ages when we should of moved forward. Don't blame the union for letting you down. You only have yourselves to blame (the union is you). Don't forget that.

Can't you see, because you don't bother to speak up, or never do anything to try and change the way things are, your life is, quite frankly, shit. Complacency is taking over, that's why your life never changes for the better. Do you know, when push comes to shove, you sheep are your own worst enemy, because none of you stick together—unless the sheepdog is on your arse, that is. Well, it's about bloody time we bloody well did, no matter whether you're a black sheep, a white sheep or a fucking yellow one—instead of us all falling out amongst ourselves and accusing each other of being racists and stuff, we should stand side by side, representing the working class of all races, and start telling the shepherds and corporate companies what we really think.

MICKY FRICK'S TIP

DON'T BOTHER WITH EXTENDED WARRANTY

In fact, I think we should all damn well meet down in London and say in one voice: MR PRIME MINISTER (Head Farmer), 'NO! WE WILL NOT BE TAKEN FOR SINGLE-MINDED FOOLS ANYMORE BY YOU'.

We should also stand outside shops with banners saying:

OY! YOU ROBBING BASTARDS, WE DO NOT WANT EXTENDED WARRANTY ON BOUGHT GOODS FROM YOU. IF THE THING WE HAVE BOUGHT FROM YOU BREAKS, WE JUST WANT OUR FUCKING MONEY BACK AND WE WON'T EVER BUY ANYTHING FROM YOU EVER AGAIN IF YOU DON'T REPLACE IT, TWATS. SO FUCK YOU. AND LOWER YOUR PRICES, TOO, YOU RIP-OFF BASTARDS.

It'll have to be a biggish banner, I know.

Now, I do feel my book represent the thoughts of every working sheep, especially those of us living and working here in Britain; and, no matter what colour you are, we all feel the same. It's the bloody News or programmed shepherds and the politically-correct brigade that cause all this 'racism'. It is them who feed this anxiety amongst us all and stir us all up. One thing I just can't tolerate is sheep being nasty to each other all the time, and usually over pointless shit, like arguing over politics, religion or money matters. This is the trigger that causes these politicians and farmers to start wars around the world, when it's us ordinary sheep who are the ones getting killed. We are all being brainwashed to hate each other.

If we start agreeing with the shepherds' explanations as to why we should go to war, remember it's us who are in the immediate danger when war kicks off. It's the same the world over—it's never the shepherds or farmer that get killed, is it? No. They will all be taken to a bunker somewhere if the Third World War kicked off. It's usually politics that start wars; they get us so fucked up in our heads that we start to accept it. They are turning us all against each other so we kill each other. That's their agenda, I think. If you ask me, wars are seen as another form of sheep culling in this now over-populated world of ours. Everywhere you look, it's apparent there are too many of us. It's time to bump a few of us off. That's their thinking.

I don't believe our world leaders give a toss about any of us, no matter what your ethnic background might be. Whether you're white or black, they will shit on us all the same. I think their aim is to turn us all against each other on purpose so we kill each other. Remember, wars are government-provoked. Otherwise, if it's not the shepherds and the farmers, it's religious sheep with an agenda which cause wars. Both generate this hatred of sheep against sheep and, sadly, it's usually the innocent sheep who get caught up in the middle of it, when they are forced to flee their countries. Terrorism is triggered by hatred, and hatred is triggered by the effects of brainwashing.

Sadly, like you, I no longer know who is friend or foe. Most of the Middle East hates us and so I have a general dislike of all foreigners now, but mainly asylum seekers that come into this country. This is something I never did care about before. Don't get me wrong, I know it is the propaganda I read in the newspapers and politics that have fed me this manifesting hatred; I know this, yet I still have this hatred. This is because, like you, I have been manipulated and which is why I now have this hatred of foreign working sheep.

Now, I understand their plight, but we are told we are getting this new breed of pretend asylum seekers, who use the term 'asylum' to take advantage of their neighbour's goodwill. This is what really started pissing me off. We were told the best country to host these sheep would be us British, and then we were told that we, as a nation, just can't afford to keep going on like this because it is costing us too much money. I'm thinking my taxes are going up again to pay for the fuckers (and so the seed is planted). My first thought now is: 'You asylum-seeking bastards, fuck off to France or Germany, or anywhere else in the Euro nations. We don't fucking want you here anymore…'

The news reports have now planted the seed of frustration into my mind and now I'm pissed off. Next, we are told that our very own shepherds are ignoring their own sheep's call to close our gates to these sheep, who are feeding on our lush grass, but they keep letting them in by the thousands and taxes go up. Then, you hear some official from customs admit on the news that they don't actually know how many sheep are here illegally. What the fuck's going on? Why not? I'm thinking, these fuckers are pinching our food, water resources and jobs and costing me, as a hard-working 'Brit', a fucking fortune. Why the fuck are you not keeping them under control?

So, then frustration grows to a hatred that is now manifesting itself into my mind because of what I have just heard. Then, later, you hear there is some slimy bastard out there who is giving them 'cash in hand' work. Now, I not only hate asylum seekers, but I hate my fellow 'Brit' for giving these fuckers work. He's probably only doing it so he can pay his taxes, which are forever increasing.

And then, if I'm not already well pissed off by now, to rub salt into the wounds even more, the farmer announces that they are letting most of them they *do* catch stay. Then the politically-correct say they need money to enable them to stay, so now they are giving them money to buy cars and training and council housing because it's cheaper to do so than send them home. Plus, the fucking politically-correct wankers have said that to deport them is against their rights. And so the twats are now taking our jobs, houses and welfare legally, it seems. The hate and frustration grows even more.

MICKY FRICK'S TIP

'DON'T DRINK TOO MUCH'

Often, when I'm getting ready for work, I put the radio on. Once, I heard that polish workers, who are working here in Britain, apparently work harder than us British sheep and, get this, for less money, and then send the money they've earnt back to their families back home in Poland. Now, not only do I hate asylum seekers *and* my fellow British nationals who are giving them jobs over British sheep, but I now find myself having a dislike of Polish sheep, too, because of what I have just heard.

I'm frightened, as I now see my livelihood being threatened by these sheep as I have to go to work and, like most working-class sheep, I struggle to make ends meet. I'm stressed, fed up, frightened and angry. The main topic of conversation at meal breaks is usually immigrant workers, when I can be heard slagging them off. All of a sudden I have now contributed in turning my fellow work mates against these sheep. Then I hear, yet again on the news, that British money is being sent abroad by immigrants in this country to be used as funds to buy tickets for their families back at home to come into Britain; apparently, we are told, it's come to light that British criminal gangs are now charging these sheep thousands of pounds to get their families a safe passage into Britain, adding to the already massive problem.

As for the Polish workers in this country, we are then told they are sending money home, because our money is worth more abroad; so they are living the high life back home on the exchange rate of the British pound to the Polish Zloty. I then look at my finances and think 'Bastards, I'm skint. Last time I let the fuckers wash my car.' Mind you, saying that they are great car-washers, my car has never been so clean. But then I remember I am supposed to hate the Polish now. So fuck it, I don't mind washing it myself as long as they'll all just fuck off home... The point is, it is pointless ranting over shit you hear on the news; it's all to do with turning us against each other. Besides, it's too fucking late now, anyway. Britain is already screwed and the sad thing is it's not really the fault of the asylum seekers or immigrants, is it? They are just trying to survive like the rest of us. It's your farmer's fault, and the politically-correct brigade.

MICKY FRICK'S TIP

TRY AND SHOW COMPASSION

So, on reflection, I say let them come in. The poor buggers, they've suffered enough. Let them all in! Come on, stay in our country for free, fuck it. I think our little island should have its doors wide open for any sheep in the world who wishes to live here. Let them all in. Come on, bring your families, your pets. Then, once you're all here, we should build over all the greenbelt land, chop the woods down, and you can eat all our swans. Fuck it, let's build them council houses to live in, too.

In fact, I bet they would build them themselves if we let them. Fuck it, sod the farmland—we don't need all that space, anyway. Our wonderful farmer imports all our food, so we don't have to have British farms anymore. We don't need to grow our own food anymore. We don't need all that farmland anymore. Build on the fucking lot.

In fact, I am at the moment thinking about taking out a large loan and building an extension to the side of my house, just so I can offer an asylum seeker some accommodation. You know, just until they get a place of their own, or move in when I'm out of work. I think every sheep should do the same. I don't mind working my fingers to the bone to pay for it, either. I'm used to it now, anyway. That way, we can be one big happy fucking family. If we've got any money leftover we can give it all away to the poor fuckers.

You see, now I'm frustrated. I hate all foreigners and I am bitter and twisted, all because of the media and news reports. This is one example how the farmer turns us all against each other and creates hate. When we are taught to hate a particular country, our government gets the backing from us to go into war. We have all been brainwashed. Why doesn't the Queen step in and send the army to guard our borders? Oh, she can't, can she? Our forces are already abroad fighting wars.

Britain is getting overpopulated because of the free meal ticket we offer to every sheep. Mind you, if we get *too* overpopulated, at least our Royals can have fun shooting the sheep. It'll be a refreshing change for them from fox hunting as that's now been banned; there'll be plenty of asylum seekers and Pols around to shoot, instead. It'll be a good game, because these sheep are used to dodging the bullets.

Welfare State

We have a real unemployment problem in this country. In fact, the whole world has. Even though there are thousands of job vacancies out there to fill, we still have sheep out of work. Funny that. You know why, though, don't you? It's because they are expected to work for crap wages, and sheep just won't do that. In other words, it's too cushy being out of work. We have a welfare state where some sheep just don't want to work because they are doing OK on unemployment benefits.

Now look, I'm sure I am speaking for the rest of the working class when I say this. I'm sorry if you are newly unemployed and genuinely looking for a decent-paid job, and that you have to pop down that social security office once a week and mix with lazy scumbags who don't even want a job, who are quite happy scrounging off the state, costing taxpayers a fortune to keep you in benefits. I really hope you do find work. But if you don't hurry up and get off your arse and find a job soon you will be branded a fucking scrounging scumbag yourself and working sheep will hate you.

It's not your fault completely, granted, because you will soon find out there are no decent-paid jobs out there, and you may think you deserve a better wage than what they are offering you. But remember, you are unemployed; that wage you used to have is no longer available, so unfortunately you will have to start over. Sorry, but shit happens, so get a fucking job.

We now live in a welfare state, but I can tell you now it won't be for long. The politically-correct wankers will deem it against your sheep rights not to be able to work, and will probably start a system whereby a taxi or mini bus will pick unemployed sheep from their homes and take them to the social security office; there, you can sign on and then the taxi or bus will drop you off at a factory or somewhere so you can work for three days a week. You will have to do it to qualify for your benefits. It's coming, mark my words. You have a chance now to find a proper job, so do it. I'm sure the farmer is thinking about this idea.

Do you know, I get a warm feeling inside when I think that it's us—the workers—who contribute to schemes like that. Yes, I'm so lucky to be a taxpaying contributor for sheep less fortunate than myself. And I mean that. So, if you have a job, then you are a very lucky sheep, just like me. Just look at the satisfaction you're getting from knowing that you are contributing to society, knowing you are paying into a well-run system and knowing your tax contributions are being well spent by our beloved elected farmer. And it's being spent on sheep who really need it, too.

We really are a charitable country; we even give handouts to those who haven't even been born in the UK. By spending a pound on a lottery ticket, for instance, you really are making a difference to sheep's lives. At the same time, you have the chance every week of winning millions of pounds for yourself. Okay, you never win, but you can still be proud of yourself, even though you know the odds are against you ever winning. Yet you still go ahead and buy the ticket regardless—well done.

MICKY FRICK'S TIP

DON'T LIVE YOUR LIFE WAITING TO WIN THE LOTTERY. LIVE YOUR LIFE WITH WHAT YOU'VE ALREADY GOT

I choose not to buy lottery tickets, but I still give. For a start, I don't care how much money is deducted out of my wages, as long as I know I am helping others. I'm thankful I have a job. Thank you... I really don't know what any sheep has got to moan about. As long as we all know our hard-earned money isn't going to waste, we are very fortunate to have the freedom to work. Why any sheep wants to be rich I'll never know.

'All I ask is the chance to prove that money can't make me happy.' Spike Milligan

MICKY FRICK'S TIP

THINK HAPPY THOUGHTS AS OFTEN AS YOU CAN

Just think what you could do with just a one million pounds lottery win. I'll tell you. With one million pounds you could finish working for a start—if you wanted to, that is… You could buy a nice three-bed house and still have change for a new car and live comfortably for the rest of your life—as long as you spent it wisely, that is. You would want for nothing. I mean, if you're the type who wants a yacht, then bollocks, you're just being greedy. No, I would settle for a million, thanks. With one million pounds that would be my life sorted out. Such bliss. A million pounds. Wow!

But I'm betting most of you wouldn't be satisfied with just a million quid, would you? You would blow the lot and be back at work within a year. Why? Because that's how you're programmed. I mean, what would you do with your life if you had, say, ten million quid? You are so used to working you would be lost with that kind of money. Work is all you know. If it wasn't for work, you wouldn't have any friends for a start, because you are from a working class background. The rich folk wouldn't mix with you, while your loyal friendships would suffer if you got rich, due to the jealousy factor.

By that, I mean you have gone up in the class-o-meter, haven't you? You wouldn't be able to mix with 'the poor working-class sheep'; you would have them begging off you all the time, expecting you to pay for everything, asking you to lend them a few quid. They would be even more two-faced than they already are. Ask yourself this: Would you want to mix with poor, working-class sheep anyway? Now you are rich, they would just cramp your style. Of course you wouldn't want to mix with them; you no longer have anything in common with them. No, you would like to experience the good life, mixing with the well-to-do lot. Ten million pounds wouldn't change your life for the better … but wouldn't it be nice?

CHAPTER THREE

BASTARDS

Being a bastard isn't right, is it? It achieves nothing and nobody likes to work for a bastard, either.

When you think about it, there are a lot of bastards out there. We've all met them in one form or another in our lives, and it's these bastards that add to your shit working life. Bastards come in many forms; they might be your under managers, or sheep with authority, or sheep *who think they have authority*. These are the worst kinds of bastards, because they are being a bastard for another bastard, who is telling *them* to be a bastard to *you*. It's all to make you work harder. The bastard under manager should realise that the bastard telling him to be a bastard to you doesn't give a toss about him either as an under manager, because he's a bastard. Of course, under managers know this, which is why they, as an under manager, mumble to themselves calling your manager a bastard after he has spoken to you. And you're right, he's a bastard. So stop being a bastard for him.

Under manager bastards are the worst kinds of bastard, because they are trying to impress a bigger bastard than themselves, all in aid of getting a promotion or to be a bigger bastard than they already are. So you can blame them for all your stress at work, because it's that bastard you have to see day in and day out. Now, the high-ranking big bastard manager you will very rarely see or speak to, because that bastard will just tell another bastard to do his dirty work on his behalf; and usually, like the loyal sheep the under manager bastards are, they will, without a second's thought, be a bastard to you.

Sometimes, you will even find that the under manager is just a born natural bastard anyway, who wants to moan at you even thought his manager isn't really bothered. He'll get promoted.

The biggest bastards of the world I want to talk about are the high-ranking bastards who have real power. You will find the more powerful they are, the bigger the bastard they become. This is when the sheep is trying to evolve into a leader sheep or, worse, a shepherd or sheepdog. All coppers are bastards.

When you pin it down to one lot of sheep, you soon learn it is these, what I like to call 'mutant sheep', who are to blame for all your shit. Remember, your fellow working sheep aren't the enemy and so you shouldn't become antisocial towards other sheep you work with. For a while, I used to think that they were originally to blame for my shit at work, but I soon realised that they were only being miserable because they were either tired or just pissed off at being at work, like me. If you really think about it, we are all just trying to survive in this fucked-up world run by bastards with authority, aren't we?

I have learnt the biggest bastards of all are sheep who work in government. Second on the list are… the lazy bastards, who live their life sponging off the state and do fuck all. Usually they smoke all day and wear tracksuits. You know the scumbags I mean.

Next, it would be the rich bastards. What horrible sheep they seem to be. You know and I know that sheep don't get rich for being nice and generous; rich sheep are selfish. Just think for a moment how much money there would be if the top ten richest sheep in this world combined all of their wealth together as one lump sum. Wow!! Now, we are talking billions upon billions of pounds. So, why don't they share it about a bit? You know, help those in the world who are starving to death or living in poverty. I'll tell you why: because they are selfish bastards. They only give to charity just to claim it back on tax again. That won't win you a place in heaven—if there is one, that is.

'We all have a choice as to which path we take in life, but can you live with the one you have chosen?

MAF

Lets talk about the rich sheep of the world

I can't comment on whether these people are bastards. They may well be very nice people. But just to make my point on how much money is out there, I have chosen to discuss these rich sheep.

Carlos Slim Helú and Family are said to be worth sixty-nine billion dollars. Okay, Carlos has a lot of money tied up in all sorts things and doesn't have it all as cash in his pocket, so to speak; but just reflect on that for a moment—sixty-nine billion dollars. Picture a billion pounds lying on your floor and you're counting it note by $100 note—it would take you about two weeks to count it all, I would guess. Yes, it's a lot of money. I don't know about you, but I can't even imagine what that sort of money looks like—it's such a vast amount, my brain cannot comprehend it. I will tell you this, though—he's not on his own on the rich list of the richest sheep on the planet, oh no. There are loads of sheep in this world of ours who are this wealthy, who could afford to buy anything they wanted—as long as it's for sale, that is.

Money to these sheep is no object. Look at Michael Jackson, for instance. He was worth five hundred million pounds, which is peanuts to many. Bill Gates he is said to be worth $61 billion, while Warren Buffett is worth $44 billion. It's mind-boggling to think how much money is out there. Do you know, there are sheep so rich that they would think nothing about buying, let's say, a Cuban cigar for one thousand dollars. That's about three weeks' work to you and me. That's right—I'm not fucking joking, there are some cigars out there that would cost you one grand, if not more, in any currency. It's a lot of fucking money, that's a fact.

Some sheep literally have money to burn. Most Hollywood stars can afford to spend that kind of money on cigars two or three times a day; they wouldn't bat an eyelid at the cost. They even have a special bank just to keep their cigars safe. If they fancy a smoke, they go in and draw one out. And get this— Hollywood stars aren't even anywhere near the top hundred rich list of rich bastards. Hollywood stars also become politicians— I'm saying nothing.

MICKY FRICK'S TIP

TRY AND PACK IN SMOKING—IT'S CONTROLLING YOUR LIFE

I can hear your minds working now—"Oh, if only..." Now, think about this. Imagine you was on just 1% of the interest earned each week of one of the top ten richest people in the world, in this case Mr Larry Ellison, who is said to be worth $47 billion. Okay, a lot of his money is tied up in other things, as they all are, but let's say for argument's sake his bank balance shows about $10 billion—that's what we will call his pocket money and it's his to spend as he sees fit. I'm talking about you having just *1% of the interest earned* on this private bank balance alone, nothing else. Forget about how much he must earn from other assets or investments he may have; we are talking just basic interest on his savings account alone. Well, the point is, even though we can't work out the exact figure due to not knowing the interest rate he could be getting, you still know that you would be fucking loaded. You'd be richer than your wildest dreams. So rich, that a six million win on the lottery would look like petty cash. Get this—you would never want for anything again, for the rest of your life, *ever*. Nor would your descendants after you for generations to come. Now, that's just with 1% of the interest earned by one sheep's wealth. The fascinating fact is some sheep of the world (and there are more than you may think) have so much money in the bank, they don't even know how much they actually have. It sits there doing nothing. It's just a lot of numbers on a bank statement to them.

Just imagine, your whole life could be one big, long holiday with just one measly per cent of Larry Ellison's personal savings. I know, you're thinking it's not fair. Well, you're right, it isn't. It stinks, if you ask me. How do they get so rich, the bastards? Again, I will tell you—it's because of us, that's how. It's all thanks to you and me, the workers of the world. Now, I know you could sit there and say, 'Well, I knew all this. So what?' Well, the point I'm trying to make is this. Even though we all know there are rich sheep out there who are very rich indeed, the worker is still shit on, working for minimal pay, being ripped off with the pittance that we do earn; some sheep are even dying of starvation, or from illnesses caused by abject poverty that could be prevented through better hospital care, while research into hundreds of illnesses like cancer are under-funded. And so, you have to ask yourself, why is this the case when there is so much money available? A donation of next to nothing from the richest sheep in the world could end it all. But they don't and so sheep become desperate. It creates hate and crime, and desperation can trigger wars. It's a sad world we live in, if you ask me.

If you think you have a chance to get rich like these sheep, think again. It just doesn't happen to sheep like us. Those success stories of how ordinary sheep rise from rags to riches are all bollocks. The American dream is a fairytale to most. Anyway, what do rich sheep do with their wealth if they get it? I still see lambs dying. Selfish bastards.

> ***You should know yourself better than anyone else, but could you live with a selfish bastard like you?***
>
> ***MAF***

Unfortunately, there are still a few of us sheep who believe this myth, that there is still a chance for sheep like us to be successful and wealthy.

REALITY CHECK—sorry, but no, there isn't. So wake up. You are and always will be nothing more than a lowlife worker to the shepherds and farmers. You'll live your life as a lowlife worker and you will die a lowlife worker. You can rest assured the shepherds in charge of us will see to that; they may make you believe you *could* be rich, but only if you work hard at it, and every so often they will even give you a chance to taste a little of the good life, just to keep you interested, but only for short blasts through your life.

I mean, like you will always have a chance to go on a lavish holiday to some paradise island, visiting places like Florida and

Las Vegas. You will be able to mix with the rich and famous; you may even rub shoulders with the very sheep I have spoken about, the selfish bastards. Good for you, enjoy the experience. And so, for two weeks you can pretend you are a millionaire like them. But you are not a millionaire, are you? Once your two weeks are over, you will soon be back at that shithole of a job, mixing with all the lowlife sheep of this earth. Yes, you'll wake up one morning and think it was all a dream; two days back at work you will feel you've never been away, and you start all over again. You start working hard, saving for the next holiday. Sucker.

MICKY FRICK'S TIP

HOLIDAY MEANS HOLIDAY. DON'T BE TEMPTED TO DO WORK ON YOUR WEEK OFF—YOU DON'T GET MANY. DECORATE THE HOUSE AT WEEKENDS IN A NORMAL WORKING WEEK. SO WHAT IF IT TAKES LONGER? IT IS SUPPOSED TO BE FUN.

When we're on holiday, we conveniently forget how much it has actually cost us. For a holiday in this country, it costs a fucking fortune and that's a fact. You also forget the fact you had to do without all year just to pay for that holiday, not forgetting all the overtime you had to do, all for two weeks in the sun. Anyway, we shouldn't moan; we should count ourselves lucky, as some poor fuckers out there go through their whole lives without ever experiencing even that little bit of luxury. Maybe you are one of those. Ask yourself, when was the last time you left the shores of your country? Well, if the answer was 'never', don't beat yourself up over it too much, you're not missing much. It's a lot of money for a bit of sunny weather, blue seas, clean beaches... You're brainwashed, my friend. Get a passport and see how the other half live.

On holiday, you will usually find sheep grinning all the time. This is because they are:

In the sun
Doing what they want
Have the money to do what they want
Not working.

No wonder we sheep are willing to fork out the dosh just to get out of the day-to-day grind. I don't want to rub it in, but you do realise that there are flocks of sheep in this world that live on a permanent holiday every single day of their fucking lives. They never have to go home; the holiday *is* their home. Unlike you and me, they don't have to return to work, back to that shithole we call our homeland, the world of the depraved workers.

Great being a worker, isn't it? When you go on holiday, you go to have a taste of the good life. If you're lucky, they will allow you to have two weeks off. But it's the rich that then say: 'Now fuck off back to work, you peasant'.

What you do have to remember is this, and it's is something you rarely think about. Did you know, whilst you are on holiday sunning yourself, you are falling into one of their traps? Now that you've had a taste of the high life, you want more of the same next year. So what's wrong with that, you may ask. It's only natural to want to forget all your woes and chill out in the sun for a week or two. Good for you, and it's also good for the rich, because that's one of the ways they keep people like us at work, and they know it. You're hooked. You can't help but want more of your addiction.

Every time you book a holiday, they are pretty damn sure it will keep you at work all year without complaint, just so that you can take your family on an overpriced holiday for two weeks each year. And when you think about it, those two weeks are little tastes of freedom; and with foreign currency being the way it is in most places around the world, you feel like you're that millionaire you always dreamt of becoming. For two weeks a year you can pretend you're a millionaire. And that's it. That's why we do it; that's why we go on holiday. Yes, that yearning to have money is the main cause of our weaknesses; that is why they started projects like the lottery, as it's just another way to dangle that carrot in front of us.

Dreaming of being rich is all we ever do. I mean, if you're honest, that's what we all want; but the fact remains, it will never be the case, Those two weeks are all you're allowed. My advice is make sure you enjoy them, because one day you will find it just too expensive to go on holiday abroad. They will make sure of that. Bastards.

MICKY FRICK'S TIP

DON'T FEEL GUILTY OR FORCED BY GUILT TO GIVE TO TOO MANY CHARITIES. YOU ARE ALREADY DOING YOUR BIT BY BUYING A LOTTERY TICKET EVERY WEEK.

Charity

Why I don't believe working sheep should give to charity.

Bill Gates is the second richest man in the world and is worth no less than 61 billon quid. Fucking hell! If he alone was to donate a half of his overall income to world causes, such as famine, there would be no world famine, none whatsoever. It's as simple as that. Now, that's just from Bill Gates. So if you think of all the other stinking rich sheep in the world, if they all chipped in and gave just a third of their overall combined income that they receive per week, and donated it to good causes, such as, famine, premature birth, or any life-saving charities come to think of it, there would still be some leftover to help in natural disasters. There would be nobody in the world dying needlessly from starvation; there would be nobody waiting for life-saving operations in the third world because of lack of money. You name it, it would all be covered. Imagine that, every single food shortage problem on this planet, whether it be caused from poverty or wars, any issues affecting the third world, all these things that just lack funding would be sorted out. Now, isn't that a thought? So don't fucking come around asking me to give to charities—ask them bastards, not me. They can afford it, I can't. I'm just a poor, honest, working-class sheep, so fuck off.

You don't have a company without workers.

MAF

If you are reading this and you run your own successful company of, say, 1000 staff or more, there is a good chance you are probably well off and debt free. It's likely you only have this due to us working-class sheep who work for you. Well, we the workers fucking hate you, with a passion in fact, mainly because you take us all for granted once you become a big successful businessman/woman. And I'll tell you this, whatever you're paying your staff, it isn't enough. Just remember that. You tend to forget who helped you become so fucking successful in the first place, you lot. I think workers should have shares in a company's success; if profits go up, then so will the wages for its workers. That way, you may get them more inclined to work harder for you and then everybody benefits from the hard work, but you don't, do you? You carry on shitting on your staff; after all, you don't get rich from being nice to workers, do you, you fat fuckers (I'm just guessing you're fat)?

Have you noticed a lot of sheep are getting fat? The government love fat sheep; not only are you paying loads of money in tax, but they also know most of you will die young. Statistics show that most fat sheep are overweight due to eating processed cheap food, and so you are expected to die premature, usually of a heart attack, in your early fifties it's reckoned. That's also great for the government, because they won't have to pay out any pension to you. You sometimes find rich people are fat too—well, fuck them.

MICKY FRICK'S TIP

EXERCISE

Do you know, over the coming years I wouldn't be surprised if our wages deteriorate even more as those bastards get richer. As every year go by, we will probably be grateful for working for peanuts. Suddenly a phrase comes to mind:

> *'If you pay peanuts you get monkeys'*
>
> ### *James Goldsmith*

Now monkeys are going to take our jobs. Well, they did send a chimp into space.

We sheep are thick. No wonder they say we only use a fraction of our mental capability. The clever bastards are the sheep who sit on their fat arses all day watching us soft fuckers do all the labour. Maybe the managers aren't mutant sheep after all, but trained monkeys. Now I understand why my boss has a face like a baboon's arse. Remember this, all you business sheep out there—self-wealth and greed is all put upon you by the shepherds who rule *your* life; you're not exempt from the programming process, either. To give credit to you business sheep, at least you try to do something with your life; I think sometimes you just get carried away with making money and forget what you was like before you was a rich sheep. You should sit back once in a while and think about where you came from. Give some other sheep a lucky break.

MICKY FRICK'S TIP

SHOW APPRECIATION TO YOUR EMPLOYEES

18 November 2009

Fucked-Up Britain (and the 'Tossers' running it)

I'm stuck in Britain and I must admit this country of ours is well and truly fucked-up. It's fucked-up because it's being run by useless tossers. It's a mixture of incompetence and terrible executive decisions. So I appeal to them, for the sake of the good sheep of our land, if they wish to turn things around they need to talk to me. I have a solution to this little problem. All they need to do is pick up the phone or write to me and I would be more than happy to pass my worldly knowledge on to them because, to be fair, the fuckers haven't a clue.

Now, I am sure you will agree with me that the country, if not the world, is run by money, but this money is being spent badly. The problem is, it's not balanced out fairly enough. Let me explain in simple terms. For a start, I think if, instead of taking all the money from us the workers all the time, which is making us feel frustrated and unhappy, they should think about giving us more to spend, say 50% more. It works like this: let's say you're on, say, hypothetically £200 pounds a week. It is a known fact that the average working sheep lives according to their means, which is basically they survive on whatever money they have coming into the house. And yes, it's true, a lot of sheep sometimes spend more than they can afford. That's why the fuckers are in debt, may I add, which is forced upon them because that person, who is on this £200 a week, is finding it hard to cope with, because workers' wages are shit. An average sheep's wages are already spent before they pick them up these days, because the farmer has bled them dry. This makes us sad, fed up and usually causes us to take time off sick, costing the company money to get the work covered. If wages are crap, sheep don't have any incentive to work. That's one of the reasons why we have so many out of work—there is no incentive to get a job.

MICKY FRICK'S TIP

DON'T BE AFRAID TO ASK FOR A PAY RISE

Being broke affects you, your wife, your lambs and your wellbeing, and that's not good for you or the country. Now, if the tight-fisted farmer and his shepherds were to give you, say, another £100 on top of your existing wage, what do you think would happen? I'll tell you—the working sheep would spend it, that's what. First, they would probably pay off their debts. After that, they would go and have a good night out, get pissed, or spend it on a well-earned holiday for the sheep and his family. If not that, then maybe they would just go on a shopping spree—buy those jeans they liked but couldn't afford before. Whatever they decide to do with the extra money, the fact is they would be in a lot better mood than they were before, that's for sure. That's all well and good, but buying that pair of jeans is significant; significant because they wouldn't be on their own. Remember, not only one sheep but lots of other working-class sheep would be out there spending their money, creating a demand.

Fuck me, Britain would be going through a spend frenzy. Hundreds of sheep flocking onto the high street, all thinking of buying a new pair of jeans. Remember, we are sheep, so look at the facts; if we had money to spend, and everybody who wanted a pair of jeans went out and bought a pair, it would create a demand. It would be vast. In fact, I bet there wouldn't be enough jeans in the country to meet the demand, so they would have to make more jeans in factories to meet this demand, wouldn't they? As a result, they would have to employ more sheep to make the jeans, shops would have to employ more staff to work behind the counters to sell the jeans, and haulage companies would have to employ more drivers to ship the jeans to the shops. I could go on and on, but you see my point? Just give us working sheep more money to buy stuff, then we would be out of this so-called recession before you could say 'baa baa baa ethnic sheep'.

So, just from that one example you have:

- Improved the morale of the working-class sheep
- Created jobs due to demand
- Boosted the economy and increased revenue for the great of the country through tax on the goods. Hence, funding the health care for suffering sheep.

What's wrong with that? Everybody is a winner. It would be fun to go to work knowing, come the weekend, you have money to spend. Everybody would be going DIY crazy, so all the shitholes would start to get tidied up as sheep develop more respect for themselves and where they live. It would save the councils thousands. How about this, then. I think every sheep should have enough money to buy a new house. If sheep had nice homes they would probably keep them nice. Do you know, there are some poor fuckers living in ghettoes, but if more money was invested in the worker then ghettoes would be a thing of the past.

What about nice clothes? It's a fact we all like to look good, but us sheep only wear counterfeit named clothes because we want to try and look a bit like you rich sheep. If we could afford the real stuff, counterfeit crime would disappear. I for one would like to be able to afford an Armani suit; I would look good in one. It's a fact—if you look good, you feel good. You am as you eat and you am as you wear. That's why poor sheep look like fat, scruffy slobs... I want to have nice, affordable stuff like a nice new car. Did you know, it's a fact that if we all had good-quality cars there would be fewer accidents and a decrease in pollution? Now, that's got to be good for every sheep concerned.

I also think that everybody should be able to afford a good two-week family holiday in the sun at least twice a year. This is because people are at their best when they see a bit of sun. And it would help bond family relationships, resulting in fewer divorces and break-ups. I personally suffer from SAD. I need sun.

MICKY FRICK'S TIP

NEVER SIT IN THE DARK FOR TOO LONG

SAD (Seasonal Affective Disorder)

SAD is when your body lacks certain vitamins from natural sunlight, usually apparent at wintertime. There could be some truth because, if the sun is shining, everything seems better. We all do, don't we? But this country is mostly grey and fucking miserable. Why the bollocks, then, am I still here in Great Britain, I hear you ask? Because I can't afford to go anywhere else, is the simple answer to that. I can't see what's so great about Britain that brings all you Americans and Chinese here all the time. It's so fucking cold here and raining most of the year. If I had money I'd have to move to a nice hot country, then I'd be happy, wouldn't I? That would be nice, but by the time I do any of that I'll be too old to enjoy it. After spending years adapting to the climate in this country, I'll probably hate the hot weather when I get old. Fuck me, life sucks.

I'm sad sometimes, mainly when I get reminded that I have no control over my life. I feel that everything I say, everything I do, is what I have been instructed to do. Like, I have to go to work every day to earn just enough to live on. I have to sit in traffic jams. I have to pay for things and accept being ripped off with everything I buy. I have to do and don't do what I am told every day of my life.

I become saddened because I seem to be the only person in the world who can see what's happening to us and this planet, and the frustrating thing is I can't do anything about it, at least not enough to make a difference. Yeah, I could recycle, go vegetarian, go on protests for Greenpeace—a lot of people do. But still that would not change anything, not enough anyway. No, to win this battle we must all become one voice and shout at the top of our voices: Baaaa!! You bastards.

MICKY FRICK'S TIP

TELL PEOPLE WHEN THEY HAVE UPSET YOU. IF THEY DON'T APOLOGISE, AVOID THEM. THEY WILL ONLY BRING YOU DOWN.

Bad Apples

I think all the woe in the world is because of just a few bad apples in the basket, which are turning us all rotten. Sadness is a contagious thing; after that comes the lack of willpower to fight. We continue to feel demoralised and feel we have no control over our lives. But the fact is, we *do* have the power to turn things around; we just need to get off our arses and do something about it. We should be laughing at them, treat them as the joke they are. It's all about giving sheep a better quality of life (a happy workforce is a productive one), and if that means giving us a little bonus from time to time, then do it. If you keep us happy, you get us out of your hair. Use our weakness.

One thing we all have in common is that we all like to have nice things around us. By giving us, the working class, better wages we could have nice things around us. We could stay in good health because we would be eating healthier, which would mean less sheep taking time off sick. Now, that's got to be good news for you lazy bastards. Don't you know, we are ill all the time because we have to eat cheap, crap food; it's been dosed with so many chemicals and pesticides that sometimes I think I glow in the dark. Have you noticed how everything that is good for you (e.g. health foods, organic food, etc) is so much more expensive? Well, with this extra money we could eat proper food like that, whereas at the moment we can't, and that's why we are ill all the time. If you want us to work our bollocks off, we need to be well fed, so to keep us strong and fit… nah, fuck it, that's boring. But we need good nourishment. We have got too used to eating genetically modified crap. WE WANT REAL FOOD! WE WANT REAL FOOD! Yes, we sheep want food that's grown in shit and I, for one, want to see a proper curved banana and potatoes that look like deformed faces and a cock. Peeling the spuds is no fun anymore.

MICKY FRICK'S TIP

EAT HEALTHY BUT ENJOY WHAT YOU EAT

Have you ever thought about how piss poor your wages really are? When you weigh it up, we work for free. I mean, it doesn't matter who you are, an average ordinary working-class sheep's pay packet is shit. Just think for a moment about how much you actually earn per week, then how much you have left after the taxsheep has his slice out of it; then, with that pittance you're left with, you have to buy the shopping, pay the bills, etc. The thing is, every time you spend any of the money you have left, you get taxed on it again and again, because everything we buy has a tax on it. That is the real reason why you are just about surviving day by day. Bastards.

The fuckers just give you enough to last the week out. Life's damn unfair. If you're a worker, by the time you add it all up, you have in fact worked for nothing because you are having exactly the same as the unemployed bloke down the street. Bastards.

We're fucking mad working, if you ask me. It's always the working class who get all the shit and taken for fools, and it's time it stopped. It's just not on. I mean, think about it. It's you— you, the worker—that keeps this world ticking. But what thanks does the worker get? I'll tell you—fuck all, that's what. Bastards.

The workers are always the ones that lose out. Why? I'll tell you why, because we allow it to happen. And why is that? Because you and I are all fully programmed working robots. They have got us good, my friend; they have got us good. Bastards.

MICKY FRICK'S TIP

DON'T BE PUSHED AROUND

I, like you, have no problem in helping some poor sheep who is a little down on their luck. I'm not heartless; it's only right to help out your fellow sheep in his time of need. You know, some sheep who has just lost their job through no fault of their own, and because of their misfortune we will gladly chip in to help them get by whilst they look for another job. It's called the dole (unemployed benefit), or social security. That's fine by me, I don't mind contributing towards those kind of sheep. Well, at least I say I don't mind, not for the first six months anyway, then I think 'Get a job, you lazy bastards'.

We must stop this welfare state. We must draw the line, because it's the workers who are footing the bill for these lazy wankers. It's you and I who are paying all the dole handouts to this kind of scum. It's all coming out of the tax payer's pocket. It's us, the workers, who contribute millions of pounds of our hard-earned cash to these lazy bastards who have no intention of ever getting a job. Scutters.

Remember, we are already on piss poor wages as it is, and if we aren't careful we will be the ones needing the handouts. I mean, what do we get for our charitable contributions? What thanks do we get for all that money we donate to these fuckers? Fuck all, that's what. Bastards. And do you know what really gets my goat? It's the fact that most of the fuckers have no intention of ever getting a job. Remember, it's workers like us who pay for the treatment in hospital to help them kick their habit if they are smackheads (and it's not as if any of them want to stop taking drugs—why should they, it's free). They just mug you or rob your house. Low life scummy bastards.

MICKY FRICK'S TIP

DON'T DO DRUGS. ALWAYS KEEP YOUR MIND CLEAR

We are surrounded by 'scutters' who bring the area that we have to live in down. What makes matters worse, they keep on fucking breeding. Half the lambs running the street don't know who their fathers are. They are all bastards.

Do you know, I think all unemployed sheep should be made sterile, and they can only have the operation reversed if they get a fucking job. Shepherds have really lost the plot; they should reward us, the law-abiding, common, hard-working-class sheep of the world, but they don't. Bastards.

Have you ever wondered why the farmer keeps you poor? It is simply because he/she wants to hog all the wealth for themselves, the bastards. When you think about it, you realise it's true. All the stuff mentioned in our demands will never happen, while there are some fuckers out there who already get all that. It's fucking true, I kid you not. It's us stupid bastards who foot the bill for it, an all. Do you know, that's what pisses me really off, the fact that, out there, some sheep are having lavish carefree lives thanks to us, whilst we struggle to live on the bare minimum wages in this expensive country. These fuckers are living it up and still they bleed more out of us, utter bastards the lot of them. Like sheep, we spend ages growing a fucking woolly coat and then some fucker shaves it off us, so we have to start over. Bastards...

A commodity, that's all we are... you know why it is, don't you? Do you know why they keep taking everything off us? It's because they know if every sheep was to be walking around in furry coats and were to be as rich as them, there wouldn't be any sheep left to do all the work. I mean, if you had a million quid in the bank, would you get up every fucking morning to go to that shithole you call work? Of course you wouldn't. If you said yes then, they have got you good, my friend. In fact, you can't be saved. The rest of you, are you up for anarchy? Me too. They don't have us all yet—come on, let's start it right fucking now... I'll lead the way. Like you, I have had enough of working for these smarmy twats who run our lives. Well, they can just go and kiss my hairy spotty arse. What do you say? Bastards.

Come on, what do you say? Let's start the revolution right fucking now. Get your coats on and let's go to London... meet you all in Piccadilly, London, 2 o'clock... I don't know about you lot, but I'm ready for kicking some serious arse. Meet you down there in two hours. Where's my coat? Look out, you bastards, here we come! Mind you, nobody would turn up, would they? Because you have all been programmed to conform.

CHAPTER FOUR

PROGRAMMING THE SHEEP

'People are like Sheep. We are free to roam in the freedom of the land, but the land still has a fence around it. All our life we get herded, fleeced and eventually we die'

MAF

In conclusion

When I talk about programming, I'm talking about how every sheep's mind is being manipulated and conditioned to a programming process. I'm talking about brainwashing. Brainwashed to do, or believe in, whatever the brainwasher want us to believe in. However, this is nothing new, as it's been going on for years, only these days it's just a little more intense than ever before.

Brainwashing, in my opinion, definitely starts at home and continues on through your school days right into adult hood. Have you ever asked yourself, 'What is the point of going to school in the first place?' To be honest, I think education is over-exaggerated. I mean, most of the so-called clever sheep I know have crap jobs, are in debt up to the eyeballs, and miserable. What does that tell you?

Power of four

There are only four main reasons why you have to go to school:

(1) The main purpose is to allow your parents the freedom to hold a full-time job; after all, when you think about it, 'school' is basically a detention centre to hold and manipulate the minds of your

lambs, to fill their heads with useless crap that you don't even know is fact-based. You are just under the illusion that what you and your lambs are being told is actually true. I, however, believe it is to prime the mind and keep them from free-thinking.

(2) The primary reason for going to school is to learn how to read. This is so you can read the fucking rules, rules that will be given to you all your working life, like in the contracts you'll be asked to sign all throughout your life. They teach you to write so you know how to fill in a loan or job application. You learn mathematics so you can understand money, basic subtraction for instance; this has no other purpose than to make sure you understand how much you must pay out so you can see how much you have left. You learn addition so you can add up the mounting debt you will be encouraged to get yourself into; if you are in debt, you will keep working to pay it off. They teach you multiplication so you can work out the years it will take you to pay back a loan.

(3) School is also intended to impregnate fear into young vulnerable minds, the fear of authority to get you to do as you're told in future, to accept orders, rules, etc. They'll tell you this is to make you a good citizen. Discipline and fear, together with the consequences if you don't conform, are powerful weapons to make you obey the rules. All the other lessons basically fill your head with useless information that has no point in the real world at all, except for pub quizzes maybe, when you're old enough to drink. I don't know about you, but who gives a flying fuck about what has already happened in history? Think

about science, woodwork, cooking, art, biology, etc. These are basically pointless subjects. Sheep have been on this planet for thousands of years and got on fine without being taught any of them. Van Gogh never went to art school, neither did cavemen ever learn how to cook. Ask yourself how many sheep at your school actually became a scientist? Don't ever think school is there to help you have a successful life or gain high grades upon leaving school on a promise you'll get a well- paid job from it all.

(4) The main reason you go to school is to establish your capabilities and to see whether you are a thick bastard, in which case they can manipulate you to do meaningless tasks (to do all the shitty jobs, if you like), or a clever bastard who they can teach to manipulate and bully the thick fuckers to work. It's all to do with establishing whether you are a leader or worker, so they can use and abuse you till the day you fucking die. You're still as sheep.

'Some sheep are born to do all the thinking, some are born to do all the fucking work'

MAF

I have seven O-levels—they are nought in English, nought in Maths, nought in science... Okay, old joke, but it's true. I learnt fuck all at school, except one thing: I learnt how to skive, smoke, fight, and disrespect sheep in authority, and I am proud to say I am the grand master of excuses. I know how to get out of hard work. I'm a lazy bastard and proud of it. I do hold a job—I'm classed as a worker, like most, but only on my terms.

M. A. FRICKER

> **'Once you are aware that you are being programmed, you will have power to stop it'**
>
> **MAF**

The first time I had my suspicions we were programmed sheep was when I was sitting in a traffic jam one bank holiday Monday, and I'd been there for what seemed to be fucking ages. I remember tapping my fingers on the steering wheel, miles away in my own thoughts, listening to the radio, when the traffic news came on. It seemed every sheep was in some sort of traffic jam somewhere. Then the reporter told us to be patient, to sit back and enjoy the music. That was followed by some news, telling me that sheep aren't spending enough and then, BAM!! It hit me: 'We are all programmed sheep'.

MICKY FRICK'S TIP

NEXT BANK HOLIDAY STAY AT HOME, ENJOY YOUR HOME, FAMILY AND GARDEN. DON'T WASTE YOUR TIME IN QUEUES OR TRYING TO SPEND YOUR MONEY

That day in that traffic jam, I thought of all the things we do all the time, and that's when I made a pact to myself—this is the last time I go to a car boot sale. So, anyway, here I am, stuck in this fucking traffic jam, watching my life ticking away. I hadn't moved an inch—ten minutes and not a fucking inch, so I turned off the engine to conserve my petrol. I sat and just continued to listen to the radio, when an advert came on. I switched that off straight away. I thought 'You're not sending subliminal messages to me, mate.' In fact, switching that radio off was probably my first spontaneous act. And, do you know, my ears started to ring. I thought, 'Fuck knows what they are doing to our brains when we listen to the radio.' I mean, we don't really know what those radio waves are doing to our brains, do we?

Anyway, so here I am, sitting in the car, and all I could hear is revving engines of other cars around me and the muffled sound of some other sheep's radio playing in the background. So I wound up the windows to shut that out, too, and sat in the muffled silence. My mind seemed to go blank for a moment; then, like a spark, it flashed back into life and went into overdrive. I started to think more and more about all the times when we behave like sheep. Then the television came to mind, and I began to question what we watch on the TV.

I started to ask myself why sheep watch crap programmes on TV, and why some programmes appeal to larger audiences than others. Frankly, I've always thought TV is all crap, more so now it has all gone digital. Most of you would agree with me, I'm sure. So I asked myself, 'Ok, if TV is so crap, what is so appealing about it? Why do we all still watch the fucker?' Then it came to me, the reason why we do. I think it's because we are all being brainwashed by TV. Don't laugh, it's true. Think about all the adverts you watch—they are all about buy this, buy that, spend your money… I know, that's the point, but you're missing the point. Think about the programmes you watch—take soaps, for instance. Now soaps, in my opinion, are fucking with the lambs' minds. Soap dramas have a massive viewing audience, of lambs as well as adults, so ask yourself: What is the appeal?

I, for one, don't like that East End London drama programme at all. I think it's turning the youth into mardy little bastards, because they watch that shit and believe it's okay to moan a lot. Well, as they see it, that's what the adults are doing all the time on the fucking programme. If you have ever watched it, you'll know what I'm on about. Yes, I hold my hands up, I have—in the past, that is and, may I add, by accident—fallen upon it when I was flicking through the other umpteen crappy channels, hoping to find at least one programme half watchable.

Some sheep are transfixed to soaps, like my daughter. I often see her mouth open, staring at the TV and looking kinda gormless. It worries me, sometimes. I end up shouting at her to snap out of her trance, but all I get from her is a grunt. Then I'll try and watch for a while, to try and understand what's turning her into this 'Gomo' and, before long, I find myself getting caught up in the programme. I immediately turn the bastard thing off if that happens, but my daughter will go up the wall and switch it back on. I tell her I'm just trying to protect her from the mind wipe.

Soap dramas are putting the wrong messages in lambs' minds, as well as those sheep with a low intellect. Adults misbehave and argue, with nasty things happening to them, while the actors play characters with no morals and what have you. They're poisoning our lambs' minds. And, as lambs copy adults, because that's a natural way to learn about life, by seeing adults arguing all the time they take it as the norm. That's why the lambs of today are wingers, unmotivated and lazy. Well, that's what I reckon, anyway.

Still on the subject of TV, there were other programmes that came to mind while I was sitting in that traffic jam. What about programmes like agony chat shows, for instance? Sheep watch it in their flocks. It's strange behaviour. Why do sheep watch crap about other sheep's problems? What is the appeal, watching other sheep relationship going tits up? They wind me up so much. I can't watch them—I find before long I'm shouting at the fuckers on the TV. All you're watching are retards and interbred families bickering. I think it's all triggered off from watching brain-numbing programmes like the soap dramas I've just mentioned. Come to think of it, I'm doing something similar by writing this book, aint I?

Mind you, my gripe is different, as I'm bringing stuff to your attention. However, to be honest, I suppose sometimes I do find sheep who are miserable bastards quite entertaining when I think about it; on the other hand, sometimes I think we should put a gun put to their heads and put the fuckers out of their misery. That's just me.

'Brainwashing or programming can be disguised as a form of entertainment'

MAF

Programming TV

I do think the television is a tool to make us all become numbskulls, plus it's a fucking rip-off. My first gripe, just to get it out of the way, is that we shouldn't have to pay a TV licence. The programmes are shit, anyway, most of them. The fucking Americans don't have to pay to watch their TVs, do they? So, since Britain tends to adopt everything the Americans do, I can't see why we still have to pay. It's fucking wrong. I bet if we looked into TV licensing fully, I'm sure there must a law under the Fair Trading Act that states that, if you pay for goods, they must do what they are said to do, or be fit for the purpose. If it doesn't, then you can demand your money back. We'd have a great case, wouldn't we? The TV is supposed to entertain us—well, it doesn't. It's full of shit reality programmes, while the other programmes are crap. The farmers blatantly use TV as a tool to broadcast their propaganda, lies and corruption. And it's your money they use to do it with.

Now, listen to me... I urge every sheep in Britain to refuse to renew their TV licences next time they're due for renewal. Fuck 'em. The Australians did this once—they won their case and now they no longer have to pay for a TV licence. We should do the same. Fuck 'em. Make a stand—don't pay the licence. They can't put us all in the pen, can they? Well... there'd be nobody to do the work, would there? Bastard BBC. (For more information see www.bbcresistance.com)

Do you know, if I did find myself in court one day for not paying my TV licence, in my defence I would say that, in my opinion, it contributes to a lot of the problems this country is facing today. I would say that TV should be banned for health and safety reasons.

I'd say, 'Now listen to me, Your Honour, the reason I never paid my TV licence is because I wanted to bring to the attention of the great sheep of this country that I, for one, believe Television to be the reason why there is so much crime. I blame TV police dramas, where the acting is that bad only lambs and sheep of low intellect are targeted to watch the shit. It is my observation that the storylines enable hordes of low life 'scutters' who walk this planet know too much about the law. As a result, you have scumbags using their legal rights in defence after breaking the law and they are getting away with it. TV is, in my opinion, the fundamental reason why there are so many unruly lambs today who are fully aware of the fact they won't get into trouble if they commit an offence. This is all thanks to the fucking TV I have refused to fund. Sheep are in danger because of TV. Thank you, Your Honour.'

If I can take you back to my youth, sheep of the jury, I don't know about you but I can remember being shit scared of coppers when I was a kid. But not the lambs of today, oh no. They have no respect for the law whatsoever. They are unruly, they are disrespectful to their peers and sheep of authority, the elderly generation, even their own parents, most of them. And I think it is the fault of the TV. I rest my case.

One thing is for sure, none of us can help but watch the TV, whether you're a lamb or mutton; it has a strange power over us. In my opinion, the moment you switch it on it's a risk to our health and should be banned like a 'class A drug'; at the very least, it should have a public health warning put on it. I hate TV, but I still find myself watching it from time to time. Well, it's not my fault, I do try to switch it off whenever I snap out of my trance.

Mind you, TV will always get our full attention because that's what it was intended to do—that's why we will sit there for hours on end staring at the fucker. It must be because we are attracted to the pretty lights or something. But the programmes on it are—and they *really* are—crap. Do you know, some sheep have epileptic fits while watching TV? So, just because you don't spontaneously start shacking in a heap on the floor every time you watch it, don't think it doesn't affect your mind; it's just some sheep are more susceptible to TV than others. For that reason, we should worry about our lambs, because lambs are vulnerable and gullible.

Anyway, putting those thoughts to one side, let me talk about what you are actually watching on the thing. Is it really innocently just trying to entertain us and inform us about what going on in the world, or is there some other sinister reason? I think the latter. It's not to entertain or inform us at all. If you're honest, you'll know it's there to control us. At least, it's been like that for the last twenty years. That being the case, why is that? In all fairness, TV programmes used to be entertaining; we still watch repeats of them today. But now… it's wank.

Let's talk about the informative aspect of TV, such as the News. Now, is it me, or have you noticed too—we just seem to watch stuff happening aboard. It seems nothing happens in Britain. I mean, you no longer see strikes or a large protest on TV anymore. Are we all really that contented with or lives? Is life in the UK that good? I don't think so, do you?

There are sheep who control what we watch on telly, and I think they are keeping us in the dark as to what's really happening in our country. I'm going to call them 'The mushroom squad'. They must be working hand in hand with the shepherds, too. I think they are told what we can and cannot know about, especially strikes. When you think about it, a strike is a little up-rising and they don't want to put any ideas in our heads. I am sure I'm not on my own when I say this, but I'm sure we all are pissed off with everything at the moment, and I think they are scared that, if we were to see other sheep all over the country who were feeling the same and staging protests, we may be inclined join them.

Have you noticed also, if there is a strike or dispute somewhere, for whatever reason, they can't hide it from the public? For instance, a postal strike or a rail strike. They try and turn the public against the strikers by making out the strikers are just a bunch of militants or something and don't have any reason to strike at all; they try and convince us all they are just mindless thugs intent on causing public disorder and they just don't want to work. I've been on many strikes and I can tell you, as a striker, that when you see all the bad press you feel you're on a lost cause sometimes. It's hard to stand in the rain, knowing that nobody cares about your reasons for being there. But remember this—they want you to look bad, they want you to become demoralised; it's all to break your will to fight. Unfortunately, they usually win—they love to see you fail miserably and return to work with you tail between your legs, looking like a loser.

It's true, when workers walk out on strike and refuse to work they are, in effect, taking part in a little revolution; like I said, it's an uprising, and the farmer doesn't like it, the fucker. Well, baaa! The farmer does have a good weapon on his side, though, and that is that he knows you're vulnerable without money; without it, you can't pay your bills, you can't pay your debts off. So, when you decide to walk out and perch yourself by that gate, they will start planning to bring you down, baby, by using this weakness against you. My message is this: don't give up. Next time you are forced to strike because of a fucked-up sheep management decision, or whatever—fuck 'em. Be strong, because if you stay out long enough, other sheep will soon take pity on you, and they will eventually put pressure on the farmer to act and give you what you want. This is usually when they start noticing an absence in the product you make, or the service you provide. Then you will get all the news coverage and support you want. If sheep stood solid we could all bring this government to its knees and make them listen.

My Study On Sheep Who Watch Crap On The TV

Now then, I've watched and studied sheep for a long time as they sit and watch what can only be described as a total load of twaddle on the box. The two programmes I chose in my research were Big Brother and I'm A Celebrity Get Me Out Of Here. Now, if both of those programmes aren't mind-numbing TV, I don't know what is. The first thing that amazed me was the number of sheep who sat glued to a TV watching a bunch of has-been twats or unknowns talking a load of bollocks for hours on end. To me, this was quite fascinating. I had to ask myself, why do they put themselves through it?

I sat there one day with them and I watched Big Brother, taking mental notes as I did so. One thing that puzzled me was what they found so appealing about it, because I got bored within the first five minutes. Then, just when the sheep on the TV started to talk about something remotely interesting, the sound went off. I thought the telly had broken, but I was corrected by a viewer who told me it hadn't, that it did that from time to time. It's the programme's censorship. So, for the next ten minutes we all sat watching the TV with no sound, yet nobody moved or attempted turn the thing over to another channel. I was amazed. Sheep tried to lip read what was being said, but then that got too difficult. Now we were watching sheep doing nothing but talking bollocks that you couldn't even hear... and then the sound came back on. Oh, hooray, at last, I thought. So we watched and listened some more.

I then noticed that if there was anything half interesting to watch, for instance like some attractive girl washing her hair in a stream... Now then, I don't know about you, but for me that's okay, there's nothing more sexy than watching a ewe washing herself, and I was getting interested in it now. But what happens? The camera is turned to a fucking tree! What the fuck... I started shouting at the TV at this point—and, yes, you guessed it, not a single sheep I was sitting with moaned about it at all. They didn't move. They just sat there, staring at the tree. A few minutes later, they turned the camera back to the girl once she had finished washing her hair; of course, so we had the little frill of watching her dry her lovely long hair, then a commercial break came on. Bastards, just as I was getting into it an all... Do you know, I'm still completely baffled as to its appeal. I really am.

I think I watched it for an hour before I started to twitch. The fact that I stood it for an hour amazed even me, but it did convince me that I was right. Half the time you don't notice you're being brainwashed by TV; it has the power to draw you in, just enough so you're fucking bored, by which time even the adverts become more entertaining.

In my observations of brainwashing TV, I have come to the conclusion there are two ways they do this, namely the Negative Approach and the Positive Approach. I will explain these to you in simple terms in order for you to understand.

The Negative Approach

In the Negative Approach, the programmes portray others having what seems to be a great life. This is to intimidate you. I also think this is why we, as a nation, feel pressurised to try and improve our own lives by working more hours. We all want to be more like them, but there is a cost. Programmes like X Factor, Pop Idle, etc, are so successful because most sheep want to be rich and famous. We buy new clothes, not simply to keep us warm, but so that we look good. It's all about vanity and status. Many sheep feel they have to have that top of the range mobile phone, designer labels, and to look good in general. The TV's main objective is to get you feeling negative about yourself so you spend money.

If we don't spend on vanity items, then we spend vast amounts of money on our homes. That's where programmes like

I Want that Barn or Changing Pens, come from. It's to make you feel that your pen looks crap. Why is it, after you have watched programmes such as these, that you have this desire to do some improvements around your home? Fuck it, I say. Leave it green, it looks all right, and it keeps the fucking rain off your head. What more do you want? I can never understand the point of spending loads of money changing styles in your home every year. Surely, decorating the pen once every ten years is quite sufficient. I mean, ask yourself, how often do you have a visitor to show it off to, anyway?

We should all keep our homes nice and clean, I understand that, but you don't have to spend large amounts of money to do it, especially those of us who haven't got large bank accounts. What most sheep do is they buy stuff on Hire Purchase (HP). Any sheep can have HP, or a Pay Day Loan. 'Don't let having no money hold you back,' they brainwash you into thinking. Have a loan, or you can buy now pay later. How many times have I got to drum it into your thick skulls, the aim of TV is to get you to spend money and hopefully get you into debt. Once you are in debt and struggling to pay it back each month, they will use the positive approach.

The Positive Approach

The positive approach is when they use the flip side of the coin,. What I mean by this is you will be subjected to watch sheep on TV who seem worse off than you, whether you are watching a drama, the news or a sitcom, or fucking reality TV. You may not realise, but you are subconsciously being brainwashed into thinking life isn't all that bad. You start thinking to yourself, 'Okay, I'm in debt up to my eyeballs, but hey. Look at that poor fucker on TV. I'm glad I'm not him.'

We, as a nation, are also fascinated by conflict TV, which is why all programmes are formatted around conflicts. We love conflicts in comedies, in soaps, dramas, and whenever we watch the news. Whichever way you want to look at it, the fact is we have all been brainwashed by them showing us a conflict of some kind. I have noticed that we, as sheep, love to see other sheep's misfortunes, especially on TV; that's what keeps us watching programmes like Kilroy, or You've Been Framed. We find it very funny to see other fuckers in distress, and it doesn't matter what I say on the matter because we will still all continue to watch the same old shit on the TV, transfixed by all the dull, uninteresting programmes, like a fly on the wall documentary or something along those lines. We can't help it because we are all suckers for programming. But all I can say is, try and be strong enough to switch the fucking TV off once in a while, if you can. They are just trying to destroy your brain cells, trust me.

MICKY FRICK'S TIP

FIND FUN DO THINGS THAT MAKE YOU HAPPY OTHER THAN TV FOR FUCK'S SAKE

Do something else instead of watching TV. Go and play the Nintendo, Play Station 2, or the Xbox instead. Read a book... at the very least, you have to use your brain a little bit. I often ask, Why, why, *why* do they show programmes like Kilroy and what have you? I'll tell you why, it's because they want you to believe that all sheep are worse off than you, and that way it will stop you complaining so much about your own life. It works because we tend to believe whatever we see or hear on telly, and it makes us feel grateful and charitable and eager to spend our money.

'And now for the News and the Weather...'

Their goal in programmes such as the News and Weather is not to inform you or make you aware of what's happening in the world around you. Oh no, they are getting into your mind yet again. They also know sex and sport sell. As soon as they have your full concentration on a sport you're interested in, usually football, BAM!! They impregnate your brain with bullshit and propaganda that they want you to hear without you realising it, like a scandal or something.

The News and Adverts

You will notice the news sometimes will come on halfway through the film you're watching; this is because they have your full attention, or the news will be on early in the morning just before you set off to work, or just as you sit down after coming home from work. You will watch it because you can't be asked to turn the fucker off, so when the news does come on, say, in the morning, we will just watch it transfixed, absorbing all that propaganda we see and hear without really thinking about it.

Adverts have a real effect on us, too. They put suggestions into our minds; for example, you may be eating a bowl of cornflakes as you watch the news in the morning, but if you wasn't eating cornflakes and they wanted you to eat cornflakes, you can be damn sure an advert will come on during the news and they will be advertising cornflakes. Quite out of the blue, you will suddenly have this fucking urge to eat a bowl of fucking cornflakes. A bit far-fetched, but you get my drift.

Anyway, as we are on the subject of adverts, just recently I have noticed they use various techniques in getting the message across in programmes, in that they tend to link them to whatever you're watching at the time. For example, if a *Terminator* film is on ITV and an advert comes on, you will see an advert depicting a bloke like the terminator selling a car or something. It's because your subconscious mind is already on that level. It works a treat because you are more likely to remember the product they are trying to sell after the film has finished. As for the news, they will make damn sure the information they want you to remember gets through; failing that, they will just keep repeating it over and over until it does.

MICKY FRICK'S TIP

AVOID ADVERTS, THEY JUST WANT TO MAKE YOU BUY STUFF YOU DON'T REALLY WANT ANYWAY

Have you noticed also, they cleverly show programmes like the news at peek viewing times, when you are a little tired and vulnerable between about 5pm and 7pm, just as you have got in from a hard day's slog at work. You're just sitting down to have supper with the family and what happens? The news comes on. The reason they do this is, firstly, to make sure they have your full attention; then, because we get bored quickly, all the bad news is at the beginning of the programme so that we don't miss it. But the real brainwashing starts as you relax, when you have filled your belly and you're on wind-down mode. That's when they start. They work on making you relax, like a hypnotist would. In between the news, there's always a commercial break, and these adverts will be accompanied by soothing music, advertising holidays or such, or selling products to pamper yourself. Now that I have brought this to your attention, you will probably notice them more, and don't think you can escape them by switching channels, either. All programmes on TV at this time, even if you're watching the BBC which is advert-free, whatever they are showing, on whatever side, you will notice they all have the same soothing theme. This happens mainly between about 6pm and 7pm—don't take my word for it, see for yourself.

The News

I really fucking hate the News. I watch it on the TV whenever it's on, but fuck knows why. Have you noticed, it's always bad news an all, doom and fucking gloom. Why do we still watch it? I don't know about you, but I forget most of it an hour later— unless, of course, some sheep has been brutally murdered or a plane has crashed, then I remember the storyline. It gives you something to talk about back at work next day. It's funny, I never remember the poor victims' names, though. Remember, it could be you they are talking about at work, and no fucker knows who you was, and come tomorrow you're yesterday's news. Anyway, that's a reminder of how insignificant we all are, mate. Propaganda and lies is the news, in my opinion. Why should you give a fuck what's going on? You can't do anything about it, anyway.

I wonder, sometimes, are we all watching the News hoping it is, in fact, bad news? I mean, I think if it was good news we would probably get bored with it. Face it, we are a sadistic lot. We can't help it, we get a kick from seeing other sheep suffer.

MICKY FRICK'S TIP

FROM NOW ON, NEVER WATCH THE NEWS ON TV, IT ONLY MAKES PEOPLE UNHAPPY, FRUSTRATED AND ANGRY. BAD FOR THE SOUL AND THERE IS FUCK ALL YOU CAN DO ABOUT THE SHIT YOU SEE.

'And Now For The Weather…'

If they just said:

'Today it's going to start off warm but foggy, then turn cloudy, then later showers will develop into heavy rain, possibly turning cold. Then there may be some hail, strong to moderate winds, and possibly snow followed by a hard frost tomorrow morning.'

That would just about cover everything. The weather forecast is therefore just because we have a fascination with the fucking weather. It keeps us listening so they can then throw some other brainwashing bullshit at us.

We all seem to watch the Weather. It's like it has an occult following of some kind. Why do we do it? We already know what the weather is going to be—IT'S GOING TO FUCKING RAIN! Okay, I know, that's not always the case; we do have nice days every so often, but not very often in Britain. I'm growing webbed feet. When the sun does come out, it's usually when I'm at work or being sheered. Yeah, thinking about it, that's usually the case. And that's another thing—have you noticed, when the weather reader tells you we are going to have one of those rare sunny days that we have from time to time, they always follow it by saying 'It's got a good chance of rain later, though'. Why do they do that? It's to keep you on tenterhooks, that's fucking why.

For example, even though we could be in the middle of a heatwave, they still have to tell you 'Enjoy it while it lasts, because rain is on the way later this afternoon', even though it's not going to rain at all. Why do they do that? Why don't they just say 'It's a lovely sunny day today and will continue for the rest of the week. Enjoy it, sheep,' and leave it at that? I'll tell you why, shall I? It's because the farmer tells them to do it—you can bet your arse on it. This is because most of the population work indoors, and he knows if they was to tell you it's going to be a lovely few days you will be tempted to phone in sick and have the week off, and he don't want you doing that, does he? Oh no. So, by the weather reader telling you it's going to rain later, you subconsciously think to yourself, 'I might as well go into work, because it's going to rain later, anyway.' So, what do we do? We trot off to our little jobs and miss the sun. BAAAA!

It's only when you're at work and you look out of your window you start to get depressed again. You look at that lovely weather while you're stuck in that fucking office, but it's too late now. You've clocked in and you must see it to the end. The wankers. I tell you something else—they aren't stupid; they know, once you have clocked in, you're there for the duration. Yet another example of how they've got you where they want you, all the fucking time. You're programmed, see? Programmed to work and that's it. Lovely and sunny outside, but they have you slaving away for them indoors, not getting any of it.

MICKY FRICK'S TIP

IGNORE THE WEATHER. THERE IS NO SUCH THING AS BAD WEATHER, JUST WEAR CLOTHES TO SUIT IT

I work nights now, so I never see the sun at all. I work all night, sleep all day and, when I wake up, it's sundown. I live the life of a bat. But you probably work in a factory or an office, or a shop, so you know where I'm coming from. Do you know, I reckon that's why they tell us too much sun will give you skin cancer. I think it's bollocks. If that was so, then tell me why black sheep exist? They originate from places where it's always sunny and a lot hotter than Britain ever gets, and yet they have lovely skin. You never hear reports of sheep in, say, Africa getting skin cancer, do you? Okay, I'm not saying it doesn't happen, or it can't happen, as every sheep's different. Some sheep may have more sensitive skin than others, but that doesn't go for all of us. All I know is, and so do you, if you have too much sun you will burn and, if you burn, what happens? You peel.

Your body is an amazing thing; it repairs itself most of the time—if you burn, the damaged skin eventually dies and falls off. All you have to do is keep it protected from infection. Anyway, I'm not a scientist or a doctor, so what do I know? All I know is, whilst you're sweating your bollocks off stuck in a factory or office somewhere, you can bet the company directors are out in the glorious sunshine playing fucking golf, soaking up the sun, slapping on the sun cream with great big smiles on their faces, thinking 'Suckers...'

Sheep are like that—they laugh at other sheep's misfortunes. Nasty bastards as a species, aren't we?

One thing that does make me laugh, though, and I do get quite amused by it, is when a mother is shouting at her lamb in the street and smacks their bum and the kid screams, stamping their feet. That always makes me laugh... I know, weird. But that's me. It's against the law to smack your child now, isn't it? Stupid law, if you ask me. I don't condone cruelty to lambs by any means, but I do reckon the law should be downgraded—if your lambs are playing up too much, you should be able to slap the little bastard. Or do what I used to do. I used reverse sociology on my daughter—if my daughter played up, I used to smack myself...

Well, as you have gathered, I have argued my case. I am, therefore, convinced the TV fucks with your brain. Every minute you watch the fucker, you are being programmed. It's all to do with conditioning our brains to conform to their rules and laws, no matter how stupid they are. Look at the facts—if we aren't watching the TV, or sitting in a traffic jam, or at a football match somewhere, or queuing for some car boot, we are either at work or asleep. My advice to you is this... don't ever fall asleep when the TV or radio is on. They'll fuck with your subconscious mind, too. You'll start to recognise systems of programming, as the signs are obvious. Here is one example.

If you wake up before your alarm clock goes off in the morning for work, that is a sure sign you've recognised the fact you're programmed.

Sport

Sport is a way of herding the sheep.
I have come to realise that, although every sheep has their own mind, one thing we all have in common is that we are all

followers and we also need to be led. Most sheep can't think for themselves, which is why we sheep are so easily influenced and believe in anything. That is also why sheep gather in their masses on regular occasions. Football matches are good examples.

Every sheep likes some sort of sport. Before I ask the question why, I'm going to tell you how they use our love of sport against us and use it as part of the programming process. Let's look at soccer fans. Now, in my opinion, they are the easiest kind of sheep to brainwash and manipulate, because all football supporters are easily led. It's only easily-led sheep who would spend stupid amounts of money on a game that involves watching two teams kick a sack of wind around a field, with the only outcome being that one team kicks the ball into the other's net. It's a lot like how a dog gets all excited when you throw a ball for them to chase—the more that ball is thrown, the more the dog will wag its little tail and get excited. Dogs are somewhat thick, but easily pleased and loyal and easy to train if you take the time. What makes football supporters thicker than a dog is they are prepared to pay for the privilege of being led.

Football supporters waste so much hard-earned money on shit, what with memorabilia, t-shirts, badges, programmes and what have you, without batting an eyelid. On top of that, they allow themselves to be herded like sheep at every game they attend and brainwashed by advertisements scattered around the pitch persuading them to spend even more money. WHY?

Because they are loyal, trained fans. I bet almost all football fans have signed up to Sky TV, too, which subjects you to even more programming. Why do it to yourselves? It's because you're programmed. Every fucking game is the same, just different sheep doing it. The farmer and football promoters are as one, basically, using you… training you. Sit! Stay! Watch the ball! Fetch the merchandise, good lads…

Come on, you Muppets! Wake up. I don't know why all you football fans don't boycott a game or two, if for no other reason than to protest about the extortionate prices you have to pay just to see a football game. It's easy—just don't go to the football match next Saturday. Watch it on the Sky box you're paying for. If they just paid the players less money for playing the game, the entrance fee wouldn't have to be so expensive, would it? Or, if that's not possible, why can't they at least throw a football kit in with the price of a season ticket for free? How much is a football shirt these days? I know it's not cheap is it? Forty, fifty quid or something along those lines. Whatever the price, it's bollocks. Make a stand, don't pay it.

I can't believe you lot just go ahead and continue to pay out all the time. Are you all that fucking stupid or what?

Most players don't even score a fucking goal for your team most of the time, so no wonder you get pissed off and start scrapping after games. Soccer hooliganism is born from frustration and breeds hate, as mentioned in Chapter Two. You should be kicking the shit out of the football promoters, not the other brainwashed fellow football supporters.

As a football manager, I would expect a least one goal from each player every match or they'll out on their ear, mate. They are all paid too bloody much, in my opinion. Give them the same money as *you* earn each week and see how they manage on that, then we'd see how fucking dedicated to the game they are.

It must be a great job getting paid for playing a game of football on a field. That's not proper work, now, is it? Money has ruined the game, if you ask me. I don't know about you, but I'd be well happy with just a *million* quid in my bank. They are ripping the working class off. Make a stand for once in your sorry excuse of a life—boycott a game. Don't let yourselves be herded this way every week. You're being taken for fools, can't you see? Just as a farmer herds his sheep in a field, only the coppers are the sheep dogs in this case. You lot, the 'football supporters', are herded and, like sheep, get fleeced every time you get to a game. You are being fleeced, my friend.

Finally, why do we like sport? Well, it is because we need stimulation, and they use our need for stimulation against us time and time again in all aspects of life.

We are all followers and we need to be led

Football is only one example, but you have it everywhere. Look at car boots, markets, rock concerts—they all have the same motive, which is to encourage you to follow the leader in front, then to spend. However, most of all, and most importantly, it's to stop your ability to think freely.

MICKY FRICK'S TIP

TRY AND DO SOMETHING DIFFERENT FROM EVERYBODY ELSE. STOP FOLLOWING THE FLOCK

Going back to that traffic jam with the radio off, I was thinking about all this. Then I casually glanced at the car by the side of me, and the bloke behind the wheel looked back at me. He must have sensed me staring at him. We both gave each other a half smile, then shook our heads in unison. Then I glanced in the mirror and took a look behind, and all I could see were cars, buses, and lorries all lined up… Well, there would have been, of course, since I was in a traffic jam, but that's beside the point. It tailed back as far as I could see, all of us queuing. I thought it was symbolic, all of us on the road to nowhere. And I thought how funny it was that, even though we know we will always get held up in traffic jams come a bank holiday, like sheep we go ahead and join the queues regardless. And why? Why don't we just… I don't know, do something else, like sit in the garden drinking a beer?

So, as I sat there wasting my life with every other sheep, my mind started to wander even more. I started to think of other occasions when we all do the same thing, you know, when we all act the same. Then I thought of the petrol I was wasting, and so I turned off my engine. Every time I join a queue, I'm wasting fuel. I remember that time we waited to fill up our petrol tanks back in the petrol crisis in 1999. I remember loads of us queuing to fill up—I think I was in that fucking queue for forty minutes that day, while some sheep waited even longer. Why? I'll tell you why, because sheep wanted to be sure they had enough fuel to get to work the next day.

But the mad thing was, as we all queued we all had our engines running to keep warm because it was cold that day. Maybe we should have all said 'fuck it' and stayed at home instead. It was nonsensical, burning all the fucking fuel whilst worrying about running out of fuel on our way to work the next day. But when I think about it now, by not having our engines running we would probably have had enough fuel to get to work in the first place. It was because we were so fucking brainwashed. No matter what was happening in the world, there could have been a third world war kicking off, we were brainwashed and programmed to make all efforts possible to get to work.

It's true. Fuck me, when you think about it, we had the perfect excuse for a fucking day off work, but no, we wasted our limited free time to get petrol for work the next day. I mean, the world wouldn't have stopped turning if we never turned up for work for a day. We could have all blamed the petrol strike, but no, we didn't because a little voice in our heads told us 'get fuel you need to go to work'. I am so convinced we are programmed—we should have just all said 'Fuck you' and had a day off.

MICKY FRICK'S TIP

IF WORK IS GETTING YOU DOWN, DON'T BE FRIGHTENED TO HAVE THE ODD DAY OFF AND DON'T FEEL GUILTY ABOUT IT EITHER. JUST DON'T DO IT TOO OFTEN

Now, what about all those times we spend queuing? Do you know, I wonder sometimes if queuing should be recognised as one of the great British pastimes, or an Olympic sport even. We would win hands down, that's for sure.

Our strange, programmed behaviour doesn't stop at the petrol stations, though, does it? If we aren't queuing at a petrol station because of a so-called fuel crisis, then the same would happen if there was a food crisis—we'd be in a supermarket with our shopping trolleys full to the brim with food—mainly loaves of bread. Why do we panic? This is crazy behaviour. Our minds are so fucked-up and manipulated that we've become stupid. So I ask again, why do we panic-buy whenever there's a crisis? Fuck me, I don't know, it's not as if we're going to fucking starve now, is it? Be honest, most of us are fat bastards anyway, and we could all do with missing a meal or two. What's the matter with us sheep? The only answer I can come up with is it's because we are programmed sheep and, at the first sign of danger, we all run as a herd.

Having you act like a herd is beneficial to the shepherds, too, because then they can predict how you will act and what you will do at various events; they will then be ready to counteract and herd you together and lead you into the direction they want you to take. In order to manage the herd efficiently for the farmer, they need to know exactly where we all are, all the time. This is so they can manipulate your thinking, once again. Baaa!! Baaa! Baaa!

MICKY FRICK'S TIP

TO LOSE WEIGHT, FORGET DIETS, JUST EAT LESS. SIMPLE!

As sports such as football, together with the TV, both have a worldwide captive audience, they use them as a tool to control you. We are all being mass brainwashed by firstly getting us all to flock into one captive area—like a football ground. Even at a cinema we are all being 'gomofied' (my made-up word, so fuck off). When you think about it, a football pitch is just like a giant sheep pen. Think about it; it's so they can keep a check on you, mate. They get you all huddled together so they can brainwash you en masse, to implant what they want you to see and believe. Implant what exactly, I'm not sure, but when I think about all the advertisements scattered about the football ground maybe it is that simple—it's all about getting you to spend money and motivate you to work. Okay—that may be a little too paranoid, but something's going on. Once we are all together, who knows what they are doing to our minds? You are oblivious to it as you stare gormlessly watching a game of football or watching the TV.

Let's go back to football for a moment, if I may. Football supporters do one fundamental thing at a match—they chant. Next time you go to a football match, look about the stadium— you will notice how everyone wears the same clothes and colours, chanting. Then, during the game, whilst you are transfixed on what's taking place on the pitch, you are then vulnerable to the programming process. Have you ever thought that that big electric scoreboard could be brainwashing you and you don't even know it?

Thinking about things like this has made me wonder if there could be a reason why we all do things in a flock, like go to football matches together, or the cinema, or car boots sales. Most of the time we don't think about what it is we're doing, we just do it. If you think about it, by grouping us all together in one space for just a small amount of time they could get us to hear and see whatever they wanted us to; we are 'the captive audience'. They could be simply hypnotising us all using flickering stadium lights, or that scoreboard. When I think about car boot sales, as an example, it could be the music of Foster and Allen sending satanic messages to us—well, you don't know, do you? We are all probably living under a constant hypnotic trance; that's why some sheep sometimes wonder whether we exist at all. Is life all a hypnotic dream? Or does it go further than that?

Programming For Conformist Sperms

I believe, from the moment your father shot his load into your mother, even from the time you started out as a mere sperm, you were destined to conform. Otherwise, why did the sperm that gave you life head towards the ovary and not swim somewhere else?

Your father, when he was mating with your mother, had no control over is ejaculation. What ram has, I hear you say? I mean, have you ever tried not to cum when you reach a climax? Do you see my point? Even when you try whole-heartedly to last longer in lovemaking, the will of the cock takes over—the one-eyed trouser snake forces you to conform, right there and then. It's inevitable you will cum in the end, no matter how you try delay it—if everything is working proper, that is. Mind you, sometimes I imagine I'm shagging an ugly ewe so that I might last that little bit longer. But it's only short-lived even then. Anyway, that's beside the point, so I will move on.

So anyway, your dad shoots his load into your mother and, at that very moment, your life begins, as your mom's egg (ovary) is fertilised by your father's sperm.... you then spark into a living form and begin to grow inside your mother's belly... For six to nine months approximately, all being well, whilst in your mommy's tummy you'd think you were safe from programming, but you're not. You see, it has been proven that a foetus reacts to noise and vibration even before it has formed into anything like a sheep. Interesting, I think; so, when your already programmed conformist mother is watching a brainwashing programme on TV, like a soap opera or chat show, you are already subjected to it by vibration and noise and your mother's nervous system. What she feels so do you. You see, before you are even born, you are primed.

Then, when you're born you learn to breathe on your own and you experience taste, light and noise stimulation. Then, ten months into your life, your conformist training begins, first by training you to sleep at certain times. It's your parents who obliviously start the ball rolling, and it intensifies day by day.

The programming progress really gets going when you are an eight-month infant child, when you are then what I like to describe as being 'tuned' into the world around you, and continues from infant into your childhood. Then, as soon as you have learnt the basic skills on how to walk and talk and how to use a potty, and once you understand simple instructions like no, shut up, etc., you are invited to answer simple questions like 'Are you hungry?' Food is a good tool to use when training a child, a bit like with a pet... The teaching of discipline and respect intensifies for the new lamb, and is taught to us by putting fear into our minds when young and vulnerable. It's all part of being trained to finally become a true conformist sheep.

Not convinced? Think of a little baby and remember how beautiful and happy they seem, right up to eight months old. In that short period of time, you can't help but love them to bits. You look into their eyes and see their innocence, and for just that short moment in their early lives you know they are truly free, an uncorrupted individual—that is, until we parents intervene and unknowingly help destroy all that innocence.

MICKY FRICK'S TIP

ALWAYS LET YOUR YOUNGENS EXPRESS THEMSELVES AND DON'T EVER PUT THEM DOWN. GUIDE THEM, BUT DON'T CONTROL THEM. YOU'RE DOING THE WORK FOR THE PROGRAMMERS IF YOU DO

We should try and save our children. We need to try and keep our children safe from this directive. We must help them hold on to their individuality for as long as possible, and it's up to you as parents as to whether that child becomes a conformist like you or not. It is you who is contributing to the programming agenda, teaching them to toe the line like the rest of us; you need to teach good morals, yes, but not to be afraid to speak out and protest. They have the right to cry, to speak out against things they don't agree with; they are an individual, and their opinion counts. They have the right to be free-thinking.

If we were to recognise the innocence of our children from the beginning, then maybe *we* might learn something from them. Don't forget, your child has not been fully conditioned yet, not until their late teens/early adulthood. That's why a teenager sheep seems to develop an attitude—they are trying to hold on to the individuality you are trying to destroy. That's why, when you talk to them or moan at them, they will probably hold up their hand to your face and say 'Whatever!' Baa!

Once they get into their mid-teens, they are well into the primary programming process. At this stage, you need to be patient and understanding towards them and be careful what you say to them, because by the time that child reaches young adulthood it's almost too late and trying to save them will be harder; as a young adult at school they think they know everything, while they think you are just an old git. And then you have schoolteachers (sorry, conformist schoolteachers) taking over where you left off, who are only young sheep themselves.

Because of demands on lambs to perform and get good grades, they have already begun to shoulder pressure and responsibility that they shouldn't be subjected to, in my opinion. They have to cope with pressure put on them by you and their schoolteachers every day, and it's all so wrong. We should let lambs find themselves, be themselves, be free to express themselves. Not every lamb is academically-minded;

we need artists, we need thinkers, we need crafts sheep. Whilst in school, college, or university, they are so vulnerable to all that mind-manipulating pressure to do well, to be the best; they are forever being tested in the form of exams, competitive pressure in the way of sports day events, homework, or the chores you give them to do. Don't ever force your young sheep to do what they don't want to do. Yes, tell them why you think they should do what you're asking them to do, but ask if they agree; if they don't want to, that's their choice.

For instance, if you ask your young sheep to do a simple task, like help you to wash the dishes after supper, and they say 'No, I don't want to', then next time you prepare dinner give it to them on a dirty plate. That young sheep will then understand why you must wash-up. Why show them aggression and start shouting and hitting them? You are just teaching them violence and to be afraid of sheep in authority.

You must remember that, as parents, you have already been conditioned and programmed to programme your young sheep and lambs. The reason why you tell them to do chores around the house is simply because you are programmed to teach your lambs to become workers. The odd 'bollocking' or slap around the head is simply a reflection of the pressure you are under to teach them not to protest, to obey you, and to always accept orders from their peers.

I have lost count of how many slaps around the head I had as a young lamb; maybe that's why I seem a bit deranged to you. Deep down, I was probably fighting for my freedom when I was a young ram; I didn't want to conform. Or maybe all those slaps have given me brain damage, who knows? Fuck it, it's too late to save me now. But, luckily for you, I think there still may be a bit of a nonconformist left in me that is trying to save you from becoming a full conformist sheep.

You may still have a chance to save yourself. If not, try and save your young sheep. Hopefully, I will help you achieve this—after all, the future is in your hands now. Yes, you, especially if you have young sheep at the moment. They have their whole life in front of them, remember that. It's never too late to change what's wrong with the world.

MICKY FRICK'S TIP

DON'T BE AFRAID TO BREAK THE RULES FROM TIME TO TIME

A true conformist sheep has had their mind conditioned to conform to rules in order to benefit the elite. It starts as a lamb and continues right into adult sheephood. Then, like their parents before them, a conformist soon learns to conform to a set of rules; these rules were set by people in power, who had a bunch of brainwashed conformist sheep or sheep trainers to work for the shepherds in the past. We trusted these fucking shepherds— some still do, but a new rebellion sheep has emerged to bring these wankers down. These wankers have fleeced us on behalf of the farmer long enough and it's about time we flocked together, to stop them fucking with our heads.

We don't know if we are coming or going anymore and have become complacent. We are so fucking stressed, confused and uptight that we are, in fact, ready to explode. We've been abused and used long enough, but eventually—and I believe the day will come—when all this shit will come back to haunt them. We sheep will flock together, filling the streets. There will be sheep shit everywhere.

MICKY FRICK'S TIP

DON'T BE AFRAID TO PROTEST AND AIR YOUR VEIWS

As I see it, we don't challenge shepherds and sheepdogs enough, or often enough. Okay, we might have the odd protest over something, but come on—a day or two standing on a picket line doesn't bother them fuckers two hoots, mate. They know, as soon as it rains, you will go home. This is all because, over the years, we have been conditioned to accept the rules of leadership, no matter how crap we may think they are. Like it or not, no matter what they get up to, we just continue to let them get away with it.

So, come on you lot, what's the matter with you? We are all guilty of letting them do what they want to us. We're always quick off the mark to moan about how we workers are being unfairly treated at work, but as soon as a union gets it's sheep to ballot for industrial action and they vote unanimously to strike, what happens? Sheep in other fields turn against the strikers. This is because, even though you can understand why they are on strike, the countermeasures from the farmer and his shepherds, and not forgetting the media, all begin their campaign to put striking sheep down and start to brainwash you, yet again, about why the strike is unjust and wrong. Before long, instead of backing the striking sheep as you should, as they are defending fair play and better working conditions for all you, you numbskulls start to turn against them. This is because you have been conditioned to attack a prospective non-conformist sheep—it's in you make-up.

So, all I can say is this is baaa! Next time you hear of some sheep striking, sit back and think before you leap to any conclusions as to why they shouldn't strike. Stop believing the media and the farmers when they go on about why they think the striking sheep are wrong. Just keep telling yourself, over and over in your head, that the shepherds are acting on behalf of the farmer, and he don't give a flying fuck about you until you refuse to work.

What is a true conformist sheep?

Answer: it's the same for every working a sheep who uncritically conforms to the customs, rules, or styles of a group, blardy blardy blah. I have put together what I think constitutes a typical day of a working class conformist. Are you one?

You wake up in the morning, usually by an alarm clock that you set the night before, then you do as I do—fart, stretch, get out of bed, rub your eyes, go for a piss and sigh at the thought of having to go to work again.

You take a deep breath, scratch your head and walk into the bathroom scratching your arse, have a piss, have a wash or shower, brush your teeth, have a shave, get dressed, go down stairs to the kitchen, and automatically turn on the TV or radio.

You make breakfast, be it toast or cereal, put on the kettle, look at the clock to make sure you're not running late. You take a spoonful of your cereal or a bite of your toast whilst the kettle is boiling.

Once the kettle has boiled, you make yourself the first cuppa of the day. You sit down and finish your breakfast whilst you read the paper, watch TV or listen to the radio. You belch, then make a comment about the news.

Once you've finished your breakfast, it's time to get yourself together for work. You grab your coat, keys and your bag or briefcase and off you go. Don't forget to have another piss before you leave the house.

You get into your car, or mount your bike, and set off to start your day. As soon as you leave your street, you are confronted by the traffic. On the way to work, you have a near-death experience or get angry when some sheep cuts you up or slams on their breaks suddenly. That's when you start to wake up.

Eventually, you arrive at your place of employment. On your way into the building, or onto the building site, you meet the same old faces who are also arriving for work. You clock in, you go to your area of work, you have another cuppa either out of the work's vending machine or you put the kettle on again; or, if you take a drink in a flask, you pour one out. Whilst drinking it, the boss is asking you to start work. Bastard.

At Work

After about three or four hours of work, you have your first tea break of the day; two hours after that, you have your lunch break. At the end of your working day, you clock out and then begin your journey home, when you will more or less have the same experiences as you did coming in. Again, you'll hit the traffic, but now you're not as patient as you were in the morning because you are tired, as is every other road user. Every sheep can't get home quick enough; we all want to grab a few hours with our loved ones before it's time to go to bed again.

So, are you a conformist sheep? Scary, isn't it? And it doesn't stop there, either.

<u>What a programmed conformist is most likely to get up to before they go to bed.</u>

Usually by ten o'clock or so, your eyes begin to get heavy and you suddenly feel tired. This is your programming telling you it's time to shut down for defragging. It's no good fighting it, so you will eventually put yourself to bed.

<u>Before you fall asleep</u> you always remember to set your alarm clock for the next day. You'll settle down to bed by about eleven o'clock, and will usually fall asleep by eleven-thirty. If can't sleep you might start counting sheep jumping over a fence in your mind—works for me every time.

<u>Going to bed early.</u> The only reason any sheep goes to bed early these days is because they are knackered from work. It's not to have sex, that's for sure; it's to sleep. That's why, by ten-thirty, sex is the last thing on your mind, and if you have lambs—ha!— there's no chance at all. The combination of having kids and working for a living throws the subject of sex out the window; that's why sex is only usually on Sunday mornings. If you are lucky and do have an active sex life, all I can say to that is you haven't been together long, have you? For an average married couple, it's once a week at best, and that's it. It's a reminder to us all that work gets in the way of any fun. I hate work.

Now I'm getting older it's easier, I must say. Now I am happy with sex once a week, though twice a week would be better, three times better still. I reckon every day would be great; in fact, I'm in the wrong job, I think. I should have been a porn star. They never fucking mentioned that as a career option at school, did they? Bastards.

If I get a hard on in the morning it's because I want a piss, or if I'm feeling slightly horny. Tell you what, there's nothing more frustrating than having a bonk on and getting myself worked up into a bother and not getting any sex, because wanking becomes boring after a while. So, now I just slap it and say 'Go back to sleep, you prick, you've got no chance till Sunday'. Talking to my cock—is that weird?

When I come to think about it, it's best not to have any sex at all when you're a worker, just take some bromine instead, because I for one have always had that dreaded fear I might get the wife pregnant again. If that were to happen I would have to put even more fucking hours in at work. I reckon that's why sheep are just not having lambs these days; the best contraceptive is getting a full-time job. I love lambs; I would love to have had loads, but fuck me, I'd be paying for it now, wouldn't I? I'd be working my bollocks off to keep them, so it's a good job I didn't. Slapping the fucker has saved me thousands.

Actually, a thought has just come to my mind. With the world being so over-populated, that's probably another reason the farmer keeps us working as hard as he does and why we get paid shit wages. It's to stop us breeding. Now, there's a thought. Clever bastards, aye?

There is no doubt in my mind the death of individuality and free thinking has already begun. We do as we are directed, we accept being treated like sheep. But I guess, for now at least, we do have certain benefits that a sheep may not have... the fuckers can't eat us, can they? Can they?

Subliminal Programming

I would like to recommend a good book for you to read on brainwashing. It is called *The Battle For Your Mind* by Dick Sutphen, or you can visit his website at www.ctyme.com/bwash/bwash.htm.

Now, you are probably aware that advertisers use brain control to get you to buy their products. So, does the TV and radio. It's called subliminal programming. 'Subliminals' are hidden suggestions that only your subconscious mind perceives. It is said they can be hidden in audio, hidden behind music, or visual. They can also be flashed on a screen so fast that you don't consciously see them; they can even be cleverly incorporated into a picture or design. It may only be as quick as a millisecond; so fast, in fact, you wouldn't know it has even happened, but that picture could be a flashed many times at you in the film you're watching at a cinema. The message would then be implanted into your subconscious mind. It might be of a hamburger, or a bottle of coke, but your subconscious mind would see this image so many times during the film that, when it finishes, you would go straight out and buy a burger and a bottle of coke.

When you think about it, we are all subjected to it, even me. As soon as I've watched a movie at the cinema, I have this urge to eat or drink something. If subliminals can be incorporated into, say, a movie, what's stopping them doing it in other ways, like on the TV or in magazines? You don't know—maybe even this book has been tampered with?

I think they use various techniques in conditioning our minds and changing our mood to however it suits them. They can put us in a good mood, make us feel romantic, or put us in a bad mood and make us feel bitter. It's all for one purpose—to get you to do what they want you to do, for whatever reason.

Look at Comic Relief week. Once a year, we are treated to some half-funny sketches and mediocre entertainment which, poor as they may be, we are still grateful for. This is because we rarely get any entertainment these days on telly, so we all gather to watch, hoping somebody will make us laugh.

And so, here we all are, watching Comic Relief on the box, all having a bit of a giggle while enjoying the show. All is well with the world—after all, it's nice to laugh, is it not? We sit there stuffing our faces, supping on some beer, maybe watching some celebrities making fools of themselves and enjoying the odd funny sketch, and we all are feeling quite content and happy, then BAM!! They subject you to some poor young child covered in flies and half starving. The contented feeling you had instantly evaporates and you, quite understandably, start to pity the child.

You feel guilty even, for here you are, stuffing your face, while that baby is starving to death in front of your eyes.

As a result of seeing these horrific scenes, they know you are more likely to get on the phone and pledge some money. Now, that's all well and good, pulling on our heart strings, but what pisses me off is the fact that there is a lot of sheep out there in this world of ours that have a considerable lot more money than you and I; in fact, there are sheep who, if they combined their wealth, they could wipe out world famine completely and wouldn't even miss the money they've pledged. Yet, they don't. It is you and I who have to pay up, using the guilt trick on us. Well, they can fuck off.

That is just one example, but I believe every emotion we feel could have been programmed by them, just so they can deduct some more of our income off us. It happens every day, but we are unaware of it even happening.

Here is a thought for you to digest. What if I have been programmed by them to come across to you as mad? What if, before they got me under their spell, I may have stumbled on something they didn't want you to know? I may have come close to putting a spanner in the works of their plan of world domination and they didn't want *you* to know what *I* know. What if they have done something to my mind and are trying to make me look mad so that you won't believe me?

I may have been programmed to write this book, so that I could influence you in some way. Maybe, if you see some sense in what I am writing, then perhaps that's their plan. I *could* well be programmed to write this book and, hidden within the text, is some other message they are trying to get into your mind. It's as simple as that and, through it, they will keep you under their control.

So, what can we do? Fuck knows, I'm the one who's been brainwashed, remember? But if that's the case, there is nothing I can do for you, for they are the puppet masters. I guess they will do as they always have done and that is continue brainwashing us to be submissive. You never know, maybe they want me to start a riot so that we destroy ourselves, as part of the sheep culling programme. Whatever their plan, one thing's for sure— you're being directed in some form or another. One way is by the means of subliminal messaging, I'm sure of it. But how do we prove it? We can't... Wow, heavy, dude.

Quick! Burn this book, save yourselves—just to be on the safe side.

MICKY FRICK'S FINAL TIP

BUY MY NEXT BOOK 'PARANOID SHEEP'. IT'LL MAKE YOU FEEL HUMAN AGAIN.

Final Thought

So, now that you've managed to get to the end of the book, always remember MICKY FRICK'S TIPS:

- Give yourself a mental pay rise
- Tell yourself 'I am special every day'
- Take different routes to work
- Remember, you're not on your own in your thinking and feelings
- Never believe a politician—they are usually full of shit
- Never volunteer
- Get plenty of sleep
- Don't trust bankers as they are wankers
- Learn to skive
- Learn the art of bullshit
- Don't take out any loans unless you have absolutely no other choice; wait for the things you want, save and buy in cash
- Don't let yourself get into debt
- Don't take out insurance unless you have no other choice
- Don't wait for retirement—live for today
- Trust nobody fully
- Don't let call centres get you down
- Don't worry if people don't like you
- Never put yourself down
- Grow old gracefully and mature like a fine wine
- Don't live in the past
- Never read newspapers. Read funny stuff instead
- Never take advice from anybody who hasn't achieved anything in their own life
- Always vote, but always spoil your voting
- Never be too proud to apologise
- Complain more

- Don't bother with extended warranty
- Don't drink too much
- Try and show compassion
- Don't live your life waiting to win the lottery
- Think happy thoughts as often as you can
- Try and pack in smoking—it's controlling your life
- Holiday means holiday; don't be tempted to do work on your week off
- Don't feel guilty or forced by guilt to give to too many charities
- Show appreciation to your employees
- Don't be afraid to ask for a pay rise
- Never sit in the dark too long
- Tell people when they upset you; if they don't apologise, avoid them
- Eat healthily but enjoy what you eat
- Don't allow yourself to be pushed around
- Don't do drugs; always keep your mind clear
- Next bank holiday, stay at home; enjoy your home, family and garden; don't waste your time in queues or trying to spend your money
- Find fun do things other than TV
- Avoid adverts
- Never watch the news on TV
- Ignore the weather; there is no such thing as bad weather
- Try and do something different from everybody else; stop following the flock
- If work is getting you down, don't be frightened to have the odd day off
- To lose weight, forget diets—just eat less. Simple!
- Always let your young'uns express themselves and don't ever put them down. Guide them, but don't control them; you're doing the work for the programmers if you do

- Don't be afraid to break the rules from time to time
- Don't be afraid to protest and air your views
- Buy my next book, *Paranoid Sheep*—it'll make you feel human again.

Our next generation of sheep are our only hope. The farmer and his shepherds are all lying to our little sheep. By using games, advertisements, the news and many other means to manipulate our young sheep's thinking, their objective is to get them all to conform, as you all do already. So, open your 'sheepy' little eyes and smell the gravy because lamb is on the menu.

'There are three types of lies -- lies, damn lies, and statistics.'

Benjamin Disraeli

How many of you believe what you see and read on the news? I would warrant a guess it would be most of you. The fact is, the wool is being pulled over your eyes, my friend. We are being constantly and systematically brainwashed to believe all that we see, hear and read, then it's repeated over and over. That way, we believe everything to be true.

'If you tell a lie big enough and keep repeating it, people will eventually come to believe it. The lie can be maintained only for such time as the State can shield the people from the political, economic and/ or military consequences of the lie. It thus becomes vitally important for the State to use all of its powers to repress dissent, for the truth is the mortal enemy of the lie, and thus by extension, the truth is the greatest enemy of the State.'

Joseph Goebbels

Have you noticed that they repeat the same news, time after time, until it is branded onto our easy-influenced minds? Usually we hear nothing but bad news. Why, you may ask? This is to impregnate fear and concern into our minds—a form of human (sheep) control, fear being police (the sheepdogs) acting as directed by the shepherds (politicians). Think about it... we are not buying it, and they are crapping themselves as we, the sheep, try and jump the fence and escape the field in order to find our true identity. What do they do? They train more dogs, that's what. And so is born is the police state, THE NEW WORLD ORDER.

Here is another thought... Earth isn't as big as you think. It's also the only planet we know that sustains life upon it... as far as we are told, that is... and it's getting smaller, over-populated. Also, the earth itself is due to run out of all its natural resources—in the year 2050, some scientists predict—and all because of us.

The combination of modern life, the lack of wars, the fact us sheep are living longer than ever before are all reasons why life on Earth is under threat, and this cannot continue. The farmer knows this. Therefore, he has an obligation, like it or not, to try and preserve life on this planet. But that doesn't mean he wants to keep all us sheep alive; no, there has to be a sheep cull if life on this planet is to continue for another millennia, and it is you, the insignificant sheep, that must be culled. If they get their way, only a select few of us will be left to continue (the prime cut).

Now, what would you say if I was to tell you that this sheep-culling programme has already started, all across the planet, in fact? Take the hospitals, as one example. They are picking and choosing who lives and who dies, while, according to the farmer, old sheep have outlived their usefulness. Why do you think old people have a raw deal? If you're unhappy, you tend to age quicker.

That TV you watch has a lot to answer for. So, for fuck's sake, I appeal to you all—turn the fucker off once in a while. Stop watching programmes like Big Brother. This country has gone reality TV mad—the reality is it's melting your fucking minds, destroying your capability to do any free thinking. Trust me on this one—keep watching TV and your mind will turn to mush, then you will become putty in their hands. It's all to do with either manipulating your mind or a humane way of putting you to sleep.

If your brain cells have become numb by the shit you watch, you won't know what's coming. Then, when they decide to cull you, you will be oblivious to it. Either that, or you will come to accept it without questioning it. What with all that shit the news spews out sometimes, I want to kill myself.

What I hope to bring to your attention in my second book is that there is more going on out there than meets the eye, out there in that big wide world of ours, and we really all should take heed to what's going on if we wish to survive. I'm talking about true reality, what's really going on right now, as I speak. Believe me, it's not looking good for us. I'm here to save you before it's too late…

Just in case there are lambs who might be reading this book, even though it's aimed for over 18s really, don't forget that your parents are already fully programmed conformist sheep. It's not their fault, so keep reminding them when you catch them doing it. Give them this book to read. You lambs and young sheep, rams and ewes alike, be you a white sheep or black sheep, you are the future and you can learn to be human again. We depend on you. Anyway, that's enough for now. I hope you've learnt something. I've got to go and fuck off to work again.

FUCKING BAAA!

UNTIL THE NEXT TIME

Up the Sheep!!!

Coming soon, *PARANIOD SHEEP*

In *Paraniod Sheep* I will give you the answer to the
meaning of life as I see it. Here is a taste of what's to come…

The Big Bang

Let me start at the very beginning of time itself so we can
understand what the fuck went wrong.

World Domination

I bet you would be surprised if I was to tell you that my
somewhat *bizarre* and *wacky paranoia,* or suspicions about
world domination, are backed up by concrete evidence. Oh yes,
it's coming alright, unless our lambs can stop it...
Custom DNA Programing

'ARE WE ALL DNA PROGRAMMED?'
We all have what they call a DNA code

DNA is deoxyribonucleic acid, a substance found in cells of all living
things. It determines the structure of every cell and is responsible for
characteristics being passed on from parents to their children.

Every living thing has a DNA code, but where did it come
from? Some scientists think it originated on Earth, but I think
they are wrong. I think it must have come from outer space,
carried by an asteroid that smashed onto this planet a few
million years ago. There is some evidence that supports this
theory. What if it had been left here by aliens? And why? DNA
is the basic blueprint of all life and, that being the case, it must
control all life as we know it. It's a bit too complicated even
for me to understand fully, but it kind of works like a computer
chip—it learns and absorbs information and then adapts. In turn,
it encourages the natural evolutionary process of everything
alive to be as it is.

The Meaning Of Life

'So what is the meaning of life all about then? Well the reason you don't know is because your not meant to know its kept from you, but your in luck because I know the answer to the meaning of life, and surprisingly its is a very simple one'.

ACKNOWLEDGMENTS

First and foremost, I would like to say 'thank you' to all of you who have bought and read this, my first book. I hope you had a few laughs while reading it. It has been great to vent my stresses and strains of life on to you. I feel much better for it now. Thank you.

Next, I would like to acknowledge all the sheep I have met on my travels and who have told me their thoughts. Everything you have shared with me has had an impact on me and has assisted me in writing this book.

Thank you very much to my publisher and all the team for having faith in my book and me. You have done me proud.

Thanks also to all the websites I have visited that have helped me put these books together in the first place.

Thanks for the Internet and all the rebel sheep of the World Wide Web who have carried out all the research and helped to find all the facts and info on so many subjects that enabled me to write my books.

Thaks to the spel checkor on this computer for correcting mistacks of my spellin

HOW MANY DELIBERATE MISTAKES DID YOU SPOT?

I think that's about it. If you haven't been mentioned in this book and thought you should of—sorry. E-mail me and I will give you a special mention in my next one.

I would also like to give a special mention to Mr Peter Stedman, my colleague at work, who not only spent most of his time being patient with me whilst listening to me constantly talking about my ideas, but he read the original drafts of both of my books and gave me good constructive criticism.

Thanks, Pete. But I got it published anyway.

Ha ha!

Thank you to my daughter, Stacey, for the photography. Love you xxx

Thank you very much to Richard Evans who designed my cover cartoon

visual-riches@hotmail.com

A big thank you to Bridget Gevaux ABCProofreading & Editing

www.abcproofreading.co.uk

And finally, I would like to give a heart-felt 'thank you' to my wonderful wife, Jayne. Thank you for loving me and for putting up with me.

I love you loads and always will xxx

Thank you to my imaginary friends—you're all bonkers.'

To my Mom and Dad for bringing me into this amazing, crazy world we live in. Love you xxx

And 'thank you' to all my friends and family and pets for letting me share my life with you.

'Thank you' to the aliens I have met.

And 'thank you' to the funeral directors who will, one day, give me a great send-off when I snuff it… Well, you don't get thanked very often by the deceased, so I thought I'd thank you in advance. By the way, I'm not planning to croak it just yet, so hang fire.

And thank God this book is finally finished (if there is a God, that is).

Micky Fricker xxx

About Me

'They say there is a fine line between insanity and genius. Well, I am a tightrope walker and I could fall off either side.' MAF©

I was conceived by accident nine months before I was born. I was then born in Birmingham, England, on 3 May 1967. I've been happily married to my wife, Jayne, for twenty-five years. I have always worked hard—until the time came when I thought 'Fuck it, why bother?' So now I do as little as possible these days.

I started writing in 1994 when I thought I would give it a go, and I always hoped to have my lucky break one day. Maybe this is it.

During Christmas 2009, I wrote, produced, directed, and starred in my own comedy variety show at The Prince of Wales Theatre, Staffordshire, England called 'Frickers World'. It was a huge success and raised a lot of money for Promise Dreams.

I've always fancied myself as either a comedy actor or a comedy writer. In my search for fame and fortune over the years, I have trodden the boards in other shows and taken on many principal comedy roles. I even once played the part of the Dame in a Christmas pantomime that was a huge success back in 1999.

I feel my experience in working with a live audience has aided me in writing funny stuff and I think I have learnt how to make people laugh. I feel comedy is where my strengths lie.

'People say I'm mad. But I tell them "I know I'm mad, so you're safe".'

MAF

People sometimes say to me, 'I bet you was a bad boy when you was younger.' My response is usually, 'I disagree. I think I was just consolidating wisdom.'

I have also, in the past, worked in television doing various walk-on parts and supporting roles (I WAS AN EXTRA). I have appeared in Doctors, A&E, Casualty, the Forsyth Saga series I & II, Sons & Lovers and many more besides. I am a fully paid-up Equity Member. I like to think I'm an active, outdoor sort of person, up for any outdoor activities. My hobbies are kayaking, mountain walking and once I even trained as a raft guide in Wales. To be honest, though, I wasn't very good at that.

Now, most of my time I am a beer-swigging fat bastard.

I like the freedom when out on my Bandit 1200 motorbike. My motto is 'Live for the moment'. And, as you have probably gathered, I HATE WORKING FOR A LIVING!!

I'd love to hear about you and what you think of my writings. You can e-mail me your thoughts at usfrickers@gmail.com

This book was completed on 13 September 2012.

Hope I did ok.

WHAT AM I DOING NOW?

Same old shit—different days.

By the way, if you've taken the time to read all this shit, I GUESS YOU ARE MY FIRST FAN... THANX

SOME FACTS ABOUT THIS BOOK:

There are 47,866 words in total in this book
746 are swear words
The use of the word fuck is 302
The use of the word bastard is 115
The use of the word shit is 77
The use of the word arse is 22
The use of the word piss is 37
The use of the word wanker is 20
The use of word twat is 15
The use of the word tosser is 6
The use of the word knob is 5
The use of the word dick is 3
The use of the word prick is 2
Ok, so I was a bit stressed. And anyway, according to
www.writingforums.com
It's okay to swear in literature. So, if you don't like it, you
can kiss my arse.
Fucking Baaa!

Lightning Source UK Ltd.
Milton Keynes UK
UKOW04f1931110615

253362UK00001B/125/P